Alex Buchman
Editor

A Night in the Barracks
Authentic Accounts of Sex in the Armed Forces

*Pre-publication
REVIEWS,
COMMENTARIES,
EVALUATIONS . . .*

"**A** *Night in the Barracks* con- firms all your worst fears about homos in the military. They have sex! Really horny sex. With straight soldiers. The bastards."

Mark Simpson
Author, *It's A Queer World*
and *The Queen is Dead*

"**A** *Night in the Barracks* is a memorable night indeed. Alex Buchman's keen eye and first-hand knowledge have assembled a collection that is intensely erotic and thought-provoking. Heartily spitting in the eye of porn clichés and expectations, the book stares you down with its hard authenticity and emotional candor. Like any memorable sexual encounter, these stories are fraught with delicious tension and uncertainty. Attractions are sudden, intense, and indifferent to politics. Desire tears through military regulations, societal morals, and sexual orientations. *A Night in the Barracks* leaves you excited, confused, and hungry for more. I look forward to future volumes."

D. Travers Scott
Author, *Execution, Texas: 1987;*
Editor, *Strategic Sex*
and *Best Gay Erotica 2000*

NOTES FOR PROFESSIONAL LIBRARIANS
AND LIBRARY USERS

This is an original book title published by Southern Tier Editions, Harrington Park Press®, an imprint of The Haworth Press, Inc. Unless otherwise noted in specific chapters with attribution, materials in this book have not been previously published elsewhere in any format or language.

CONSERVATION AND PRESERVATION NOTES

All books published by The Haworth Press, Inc. and its imprints are printed on certified pH neutral, acid free book grade paper. This paper meets the minimum requirements of American National Standard for Information Sciences-Permanence of Paper for Printed Material, ANSI Z39.48-1984.

A Night in the Barracks
Authentic Accounts of Sex in the Armed Forces

HARRINGTON PARK PRESS
New, Recent, and Forthcoming Titles
of Related Interest

The Bear Book: Readings in the History and Evolution of a Gay Male Subculture edited by Les Wright

The Bear Book II: Further Readings in the History and Evolution of a Gay Male Subculture edited by Les Wright

Bad Boys and Tough Tattoos: A Social History of the Tattoo with Gangs, Sailors, and Street-Corner Punks, 1950-1965 by Samuel M. Steward

Barrack Buddies and Soldier Lovers: Dialogues with Gay Young Men in the Military by Steven Zeeland

Sailors and Sexual Identity: Crossing the Line Between "Straight" and "Gay" in the U.S. Navy by Steven Zeeland

Rarely Pure and Never Simple: Selected Essays of Scott O'Hara by Scott O'Hara

It's a Queer World: Deviant Adventures in Pop Culture by Mark Simpson

Military Trade by Steven Zeeland

When It's Time to Leave Your Lover: A Guide for Gay Men by Neil Kaminsky

Male Lust: Pleasure, Power, and Transformation edited by Kerwin Kay, Jill Nagle, and Baruch Gould

Tricks and Treats: Sex Workers Write About Their Clients edited by Matt Bernstein Sycamore

The Mentor: A Memoir of Friendship and Gay Identity by Jay Quinn

Infidelity by William Rooney

Rooney's Shorts by William Rooney

Love, the Magician by Brian Bouldrey

Rebel Yell: Stories by Contemporary Southern Gay Authors edited by Jay Quinn

Growing Up Gay in the South: Race, Gender, and Journeys of the Spirit, Tenth Anniversary Edition by James T. Sears

A Night in the Barracks
Authentic Accounts of Sex in the Armed Forces

Alex Buchman
Editor

Southern Tier Editions
Harrington Park Press®
An Imprint of The Haworth Press, Inc.
New York • London • Oxford

Published by

Southern Tier Editions, Harrington Park Press®, an imprint of The Haworth Press, Inc., 10 Alice Street, Binghamton, NY 13904-1580

© 2001 by The Haworth Press, Inc. All rights reserved. No part of this work may be reproduced or utilized in any form or by any means, electronic or mechanical, including photocopying, microfilm, and recording, or by any information storage and retrieval system, without permission in writing from the publisher. Printed in the United States of America.

Cover design by Jennifer M. Gaska.

Cover photo © The Body Shoppe / <www.tbs-thebodyshoppe.com>.

Back cover photo of Alex Buchman © Steven Zeeland / <www.seadogphoto.com>.

Depiction or mention of any person in this work should not be construed as an implication of said person's sexual orientation.

The Library of Congress has cataloged the hardcover edition of this book as:

Buchman, Alex.
　A night in the barracks : authentic accounts of sex in the Armed Forces / Alex Buchman.
　　p. cm.
　ISBN 1-56023-987-5 (hard : alk. paper)—ISBN 1-56023-988-3 (soft : alk. paper)
　1. United States—Armed Forces—Gays—Sexual behavior—Anecdotes. I. Title.

UB418.G38 B83 2000
306.76'62—dc21
　　　　　　　　　　　　　　　　　　　　　　　　　　　　　　　00-033530

To
Tony Beatown Saint of Sailors,
Neil and Chris and Edith Prickley,
M. Mau,
and Keith

CONTENTS

ABOUT THE EDITOR

Alex Buchman is a former United States Marine. He served during the Gulf War, and was honorably discharged. Currently, he makes his home in San Diego, California, where he is already at work on a sequel to this collection.

Foreword

Message in a Bottle

In "gay" erotica, no backdrop has proven more enduring than the barracks. From a soldier-hustler's memoir called *The Sins of the Cities of the Plains* published in 1889 (three years before the word *heterosexual* was coined), to the 1950s glory days of the Athletic Model Guild, on down to the "true-life" tearoom-wall testaments of Boyd McDonald and his lesser, present-day imitators, the masculine world of the barracks has remained a gay porn staple, as steadfastly seductive a setting as locker rooms, fraternity houses, and jail cells.

With this anthology, Alex Buchman has succeeded in giving a time-honored genre a fresh new twist. Himself a former U.S. Marine, Buchman has assembled a collection that is no less tantalizing than the best of its predecessors, and appreciably more *authentic*.

To be sure, some readers may be taken off guard that not every participant here boasts a gargantuan penis, and not every encounter ends in a picture-perfect money shot. The sexual situations recounted are sometimes awkward, frustrating, even heartbreaking. But ultimately, these stories are hotter than any fiction because they are so thrillingly, achingly real. In this post-postmodern era of digital enhancement, where even sexual identity itself may soon appear on the electronic auction block, authenticity is something you can put your hand around.

* * *

Most post-Stonewall military-theme gay porn, of course, has little to do with any actual barracks experience and everything to do with a utopian fantasy of a fraternal community in which all soldiers and sailors are "real men" and at the same time "really gay." Seventies pulp novels in particular have provided rich fodder for recent scathing commentaries by sanctimonious *Gay* writers who preach that any *Gay* pornography set outside of urban *Gay* ghettoes necessarily amounts to "fawning over the virility of *straight* men," and is therefore damning evidence of "fundamental self-loathing." *Pre*-Stonewall pornography, it almost goes without saying, is equivalent to the Stone Age.

In *Hard to Imagine: Gay Male Eroticism in Photography and Film From Their Beginnings to Stonewall* (Columbia, 1996), Thomas Waugh, the preeminent scholar of gay porn imagery, offers a more nuanced approach. Waugh observes that 1950s "physique" films were

> an embodiment, not of the secret rites of an underground subculture . . . but of belonging to the mainstream of homo-social normalcy. The narrative content of this myth is the rituals of patriarchal power, especially the violent male bonding of sports (or combat or manual work, etc.). When eroticized, this violent bonding takes on a sadomasochistic dynamic, invariably with the invisible spectator entering only as a bottom.

Waugh's contention that the consumer of such images can never "enter" into these narrratives in an *active* way is open to question. What never ceases to amaze and delight me are the endlessly enterprising ways in which individual human animals manage to get their cultural cues *wrong,* and take creative liberties they may not even be aware of *not* being permitted. (I think of a Marine I know who once off-handedly referred to his [yes, in this case it actually was Tom-of-Finland gargantuan] erection as "she." When I quizzed him about why he thought of his penis in this way, he looked at me with bewilderment and alarm.

"Doesn't everybody?" Pressed further, he sputtered, "But, but—it's sleek and long, like a ship. And ships are always called 'she.' " How could I argue with that?)

But Waugh also acknowledges that, in focusing so tightly on homosocial spaces, 1950s gay erotica not only spotlights "the mainstream sancrosanctity of military, athletic, workplace, and educational institutions," but *"the ambiguous border zones between the homosocial and the homosexual in general"* [my emphasis. My raison d'être].

Buchman presents his stories for their value as sexy, entertaining reading, and not with any pretense of scholarly significance. But to the student of same-sex desire in institutional all-male milieux, the unvarnished surfaces of this boldly convention-defying "hands-on" exhibit promise to inflict some exquisitely piercing slivers of insight into precisely these border zones.

Consider Tim Bergling's story "Sex As a Weapon." His title refers to the battle between the homoerotically charged homosocial and the self-consciously *other* homosexual. Marine corporals Tim and Rick are best buddies; they go everywhere and do (almost) everything together. But Tim's burgeoning awareness of "who he really is" impels him to confront his straight pal with "a triple whammy." In breathless succession he informs Rick: (1) I'm a different sexual species from you; (2) I want you like you want women; (3) I want you to prostitute yourself to my tonsils. Is it really any surprise that, upon being hit with this, Tim's macho Marine roommate breaks down in tears? The gay Marine gets his wish; indeed, he experiences a rapture "akin to the unwrapping of the ultimate Christmas present." But he is forever expelled from the homosocial Eden of barrack buddyship.

"Semen in a Bullet" chronicles a barracks romance that starts off seemingly in echo of "Sex As a Weapon," but turns out very differently. Scott and his best straight buddy are caught in the act, in the middle of the Gulf War—in the middle of a tent full of sleeping gung-ho Army Rangers. Ironically, of the two men seen and heard initiating sodomy, it was Scott's partner Hank—the straight-identified top man—who was subsequently harassed, and even then only mildly. Scott's account appears to fit a body of post–World War II historical evidence that illustrates some of the conditions under which sexual behavior between men can sometimes become known of and tacitly accepted *on the unit level:* (1) among men who have already proven their masculinity, in an environment where sexually available women either are not present or are strategically ignored; (2) in wartime, when men are cognizant that any night and any intimate contact could be their last; and (3) when one or more of the participants is someone to whom even the most "homophobic" serviceman is obliged to bow down to. As the company supply clerk, Scott was in a position to make things difficult for any soldier in his unit who dared treat him with open disrespect.

In "Barracks Gang Bang," Gayle Martin shares her story of what, for many military admirers, could be the ultimate fantasy: on-base sex with an endless onslaught of sex-starved Marine infantrymen, average age nineteen, lining up at 3 a.m. as if summoned for alert, half-asleep, half-dressed, more than half of them unabashedly half-hard. Putting aside the fact that, under the Uniform Code of Military Justice, the outgoing Commander in Chief at the time of this writing is himself a certified sodomite, all the sexual acts Gayle recounts are heterosexual. But there is no overlooking the glaring "homosexual" subtext. One Marine can't get an erection—*because his buddies are present,* he claims (cluelessly, as it is evident that he has only been included in a benevolent but hopeless effort to transform him from a nerdy misfit "kid brother" into a unit-cohesive "hard" Devil Dog). Another draws the line at kissing Gayle after she has fellated his buddy. But a third Marine happily, even hungrily transgresses this boundary. Gayle's body is of secondary interest to these young men; their primary concern is sexually consummating their bond with each other. As Gayle observes, "They were just too comfortable laughing and joking when saying, 'Get your dick out of my face.'"

Mantra-like, I can only repeat the mundane fact of life that Alfred Kinsey daringly spelled out to America more than fifty years ago: "Males do not represent two discrete populations, heterosexual and homosexual. The world is not to be divided into sheep and goats. Not all things are black nor all things white." It may be worth adding that typically, when people question the validity of Dr. Kinsey's research, they complain that he relied too much on data he collected from men in institutional settings—such as prisons, fraternity houses, and the military.

*   *   *

A year or two ago, *Out* magazine published a whimsical suggested reading list for the U.S. Vice President. Included was my own *Barrack Buddies,* with the punch line: "Let's confirm their worst fears." And indeed, some gays will likely continue to spout knee-jerk accusations that books such as these risk undermining a carefully scripted advertising cam–paign aimed at persuading the U.S. public that gays in the military are all clean-cut disease-free superpatriotic superperformers who never have sex outside of middle class off-base bedrooms. What these well-intentioned good-gay evangelists steadfastly fail to *get* is that the U.S. public can never be propagandized into imagining that sailors with a taste for sex between men are all sort of smiling asexual earthworms who, during a six-month cruise, will never even think about sex. The *first* thing that "straights" are likely to think of when confronted with the image of sodomite submariners is, "What goes where?" (In many cases, they are also likely to recall certain of their own uncomfortable category-defying secret desires, felt in waking life or in dreams—desires that the gay movement cluelessly preaches can only be felt *authentically* by the tiny proportion of the population that "has no choice about who they *really* are.")

News flash: an unknowable, incalculable, ever-shifting percentage of military men experience feelings that may or may not fit somebody or other's notions of what might or might not pass muster as *authentic* same-sex desire. Some of them end up identifying themselves as gay. Most of them do not. Ironically, gays are often more unnerved by sexual tension in the barracks than their comrades, and are less likely to participate in homoerotic high jinks. Real life barracks can sometimes, in some ways, surpass the most outlandish gay porn fantasy. But sex with or between military men may not always meet the exacting standards of what "gays" deem genuinely *Gay* sex. As an embittered former servicemen hissed in an anonymous "reader review" of *Sailors and Sexual Identity* posted to an online bookseller: "Zeeland would have the reader believing that there's no such thing as a straight boy on a ship that's underway. His book simply panders to the lustful fantasies of those who haven't had the opportunity to live with a bunch of uneducated, mindless slobs 90 percent of whom never even *heard* of Barbra Streisand!"

Somewhere, sometime in the future, someone reading this will look back on the issue of "gays in the military" as *so* twentieth century. In the meantime, I hope you will enjoy the stories Alex Buchman has collected documenting how some real-life soldiers, sailors, airmen, Marines, and even one Coast Guardsman connected sexually with other men despite or because they weren't supposed to.

Steven Zeeland
Bremerton, Washington

Preface

Porno from Camp Horno

For four years I served in the United States Marine Corps. During this period, I had ample opportunity to experience many aspects of life in the Corps. From short-term assignments in tight Navy berthing areas to wet and cold extended field exercises with the grunts, I saw, did, and learned a lot—both about myself and my fellow Marines. Most relevant for this book, I had my first sexual experiences with men. Civilians, sailors, and other Marines.

Like a lot of other men, porn played a big part in my coming-out experience. I was stationed on Camp Pendleton. The nearest big city was San Diego, and one weekend when I was down there I stopped in an adult bookstore. As I looked through the various jugs-and-butts magazines, a magazine a few shelves over caught my eye. On the cover was a brawny, short-haired man, naked on a forklift. I was at first intensely aroused, then ashamed. Then I realized that I needed that magazine. I convinced myself on the car ride back to base that what I was doing wasn't wrong. But back in the barracks, after tearing off the shrink-wrap and looking at all the pictures of the men, my desire faded. The pictures inside didn't live up to the cover. I felt not only guilty, but cheated.

On my next visit to the store I picked up a gay erotica paperback, a "fuck book." I picked it out because they were stories about the military. I wanted to have sex with other sailors and Marines, but so far I hadn't. Up until that point, I had only had sex with Asian female prostitutes.

The book was mainly written by a supposed naval officer. The stories I liked best were about him having sex with Marines. It almost seemed like he worshipped Marines. The stories seemed almost believable enough to me, even if they were a little bit over the top. But they were a little bit too perfect to be real.

After I came out and started going to bars and bathhouses I met a sailor named Tom. Through him I met Steve Zeeland, who ended up interviewing me under the pseudonym "Alex" for his book *The Masculine Marine: Homoeroticism in the U.S. Marine Corps.*

Eventually Steve and I became roommates. When he snooped through my stuff and came across that military porn book of course he quizzed me about when, where, and why I bought it. He seemed to think there was something funny about the fact that I'd held onto it. Later on, when someone would send Steve military sex stories, he sometimes gave them to me to read. He was curious to see what I'd have to say about their authenticity. But it was also interesting to him that stuff like that worked for me. For me, written erotica is a lot more arousing than just staring at a picture. Steve is pretty much the opposite. He gets off on pictures, not words.

A little over twelve months ago, he suggested that I would be more qualified than he to edit an anthology of military erotica. I decided that it might be fun to edit my own book. Together, we got in touch with friends and other contacts he'd made through book readings, and we posted a general call for submissions to his Web site. Steve dumped off on me two banker's boxes of stuff he'd put aside—stacks of "true encounter" letters sent by readers/fans/whatever, outtakes from his own manuscripts; even a few raw interview tapes that Steve had never bothered to transcribe because, he said, the guys on them wouldn't (or couldn't) "open up about their backgrounds, their day-to-day military lives—blah, blah, blah. All they wanted to talk about was their sexual conquests."

This is what I came up with.

I wanted to make the book a more human and more accurate representation of what sex in the military is all about. Some of the stories may not be as fantasy-fulfilling as some people might want from a book like this, but each chapter offers its own individual erotic perspective on life in the military.

How do I know these stories are any truer than those in *Penthouse Forum?* Most of the contributors are people that I or Steve have had enough contact with to be reasonably confident of their credibility. Some of the language in the submissions may be choppy or crude, but I have not greatly altered this in order to preserve the "militaryspeak." Anyone who has ever spent any time with military personnel will know that this is the way they talk, and write.

I want people to get from this book generally that not all eroticism of the military is based on big dicks and hot sex. Flaws, frustrations, and foiled once-in-a-lifetime chances to make fantasies come true can also be part of what makes a story erotically charged. Nowadays, as a civilian who hangs out in leather bars from New York to Rome, I've found that my gay male friends and acquaintances are usually disappointed with most of my Marine stories. They can't stand it that the stories always start with a sexually tense situation, but don't usually end in what they consider a satisfying sexual climax. One of my friends even suggested that I should just lie and change the endings to tell people what they want to hear. But I have to admit I get a certain thrill from continuing to tell the stories exactly as they happened.

My own story, "Tank Trail," which closes this book, is one of the few almost "perfect" erotic experiences I had in the Marine Corps. Believe it or not, there really is an area of Camp Pendleton called Camp Horno.

This is book is not social science. It's "erotica." But I hope that it might help broaden your erotic fantasies to include a little more of what military men's experiences are really like. If you have stories and you'd like to contribute to possible future volumes, please write me in care of The Haworth Press.

Alex Buchman
San Diego, California

–1–

Sex As a Weapon

Tim Bergling

There was music playing, some mid-1980s pop confection called "Object of My Desire." A great little dance tune, actually, but dancing wasn't what I had in mind right then, wedged sideways as I was in the front seat of Rick's car, my face hovering over his crotch.

"Are you sure?" I asked him one last time as he lay back and cocked the driver's seat into its full reclining position. "Because if you're not sure, we'll just stop right now, and tomorrow we'll tell each other how drunk we were last night, or some such lame bullshit, and pretend that none of this ever happened."

I was trying hard to keep the desperate edge off of my voice, but it was a pretty dismal attempt. Rick was no fool; he knew I wanted him, and wanted him bad. By now, how could he not know? I'd waited so long for this moment, never dreaming it might actually happen, that I thought I was about to explode; still it didn't mean I had to give him any more satisfaction than one usually gets with a really good blow job. His ego, at least, didn't need any more stroking that night.

But Rick was in an amiable mood, a welcome by-product of all that cheap wine we'd been guzzling for the past hour or so. "Go ahead," he said, his voice strangely muffled in the intimate acoustics of his 280Z. "But I gotta tell you, Tim. I really don't think you're gonna be able to get me off. Blow jobs are a great appetizer; they're not, like, the main course, if you know what I'm sayin'."

1

"That's 'cause you've been wasting your time with girls who don't know what they're doing," I assured him as I undid his belt buckle. "Only a guy can really do another guy."

A pause, then a snort, perhaps of disapproval that I could be so casually dismissive of the young ladies whose attentions, oral and otherwise, he spent his time pursuing. "Yeah, whatever."

The belt dispatched with, I popped open his fly button and slowly unzipped his jeans. In all of life's experiences there's nothing that quite matches a moment like that. It's something akin to the unwrapping of the ultimate Christmas present, if you could somehow manage to place all of your passion, desire, lust—and yes, your love—into a brightly colored box with a bow on top. How you want to rip through all that gift wrapping and get to what lies beneath, while simultaneously wishing you could freeze the scene into a living, breathing photograph, and have it to hold close forever . . . to recall the excruciating anticipation, the feel of your young, unbroken heart pounding in your head . . . to remember how your very respiration grew thin and labored, and your entire world narrowed to the sight in front of you.

I couldn't take it anymore, and I slid his jeans down over his smooth, muscular thighs, legs that still showed a tan from a summer sun that seemed like, what, a hundred years before? So much had come and gone since. It was hard to believe all the roads of seasons past had led us here to this unexpected coupling. Now with his pants gathered in a bunch above his ankles, his white briefs a glowing blue triangle in the surprisingly bright light cast from the digital clock on the dash, Rick might have looked ridiculous. But he did not. He was Love Incarnate to me.

Yet the modest bulge inside his jockeys seemed to indicate that, for his part, Rick wasn't quite turned on by our novel situation. That stood to change, I wagered, and very soon. I lowered my face against him, probing the hidden contours with my forehead and nose. All these months, and now only a thin veil of 100 percent cotton remained between me and—Oh, the hell with it, I thought.

With a suddenness that probably took us both by surprise, I straightened up slightly, grasped his shorts with both hands, and slid them down to meet his jeans. I paused to admire the view.

That song was still playing, and I had to smile despite myself. Object of my desire, indeed.

*   *   *

Rick and I were United States Marines—both of us corporals—stationed in Quantico, Virginia. Our home was the Presidential Helicopter Squadron, known by its official military designation as HMX-1. You've doubtless seen the unit's showpiece on television. There's the sharp-looking Marine decked out in full dress blue uniform, snapping to attention and smartly saluting the Commander in Chief as he lopes down the steps of Marine One with numerous aides and the First Lady in tow.

I wish I could claim that one or both of us had on occasion been that particular sharp-looking Marine, and from ten years on I guess it would be a cool fib to tell, but the truth is less glamorous. I worked in Squadron Administration, keeping our people paid and promoted on time; Rick was in Supply, where he helped to make sure the Squadron's birds stayed up in the air when they were supposed to, that their myriad of parts were kept clean and intact. Neither of us ever made the network news, but we were nonetheless hard-charging Marine NCOs, in vital-if-obscure supporting positions.

Rick and I had become fast friends shortly after I arrived at the Squadron. Nothing too unusual about that; military life is a lot like college, much more than most people would ever imagine. Just substitute the barracks for the dorm, and the job you do every day for going to class, and there you are. The vibe is pretty much the same, the major differences being, of course, that the environment is overwhelmingly male, and that few people ever ditch their job because of a drinking binge the night before.

And, just like at your average college, bonds of friendship in the military often grow deeper and more rapidly than those outside the ivy-covered walls, or in our case, the barbed-wire fence. Looking back now, it's all sort of a blur, and it seems virtually all my buddies and I progressed from introductions to intimacy in the blink of a jarhead's eye.

I came to know Rick's face and physique long before I ever learned his name. He was, after all, the quarterback on the Squadron's football team, the lead-off hitter on the softball roster, and a frequent contestant in the various boxing matches thrown together by the Base Recreation Department. I'd sort of admired him from afar, and I'd certainly enjoyed watching him play, but the different circles we traveled in never seemed to intersect.

Fate arrived one warm spring day in the form of a sudden thunderstorm that caught me walking along the road to the softball field. I was on the way to take in a game when all hell broke loose from above. A hundred yards from the nearest shelter, I'd just resigned myself to getting soaked when a car pulled up alongside me in a spray of gravel and mud. The door flew open; the driver wanted to know if needed a ride.

It was Rick. Our encounter lasted maybe ten minutes, from the time he picked me up to the time he dropped me off back at my barracks, but suffice to say he made quite an impression in the dry and cozy confines of the very car in which I would later find my Nirvana. I was smitten.

Not long after that, through various wheelings and dealings too arcane to delve into here, I was freed from my bondage at one of the worst military organizations known to man, Quantico's Officer Candidates School, and assigned to HMX-1. Upon moving into my new barracks digs, whom would I happen to discover living right across the squadbay but my handsome rescuer from the rain. His entrance was vivid and memorable. There I was, surveying my new surroundings, standing with all my worldly possessions crammed into a seabag and several boxes, and wondering just where the fuck I was going to put everything, when I glanced up to see Rick in all his buck-naked glory, posed by his wall locker and combing his jet-black hair in a tiny mirror. A small towel was thrown cavalierly across one well-tanned shoulder but, trust me, it covered nothing of any importance. It was everything I could do not to drop my stuff and stare.

"Hey, man," he called out cheerfully. "You moving in?"

"Uh, yeah, I guess so," I answered, somewhat at a loss for words. He looked so hot standing there, like a page torn from someone's Dream Guy calendar; just a bit shorter than my five-feet-eleven, smooth and muscular from his broad shoulders to his powerful legs. He turned toward his mirror from time to time as we spoke, allowing me to take in details still etched firmly in my memory: a handsome, all-American face, as if he'd fallen off the nearest recruiting poster; a fine, rounded chest; narrow hips, and the firmest, tightly rounded butt I've ever seen. Not a body hair in sight, except—well, I tried not to look, but I had to, you know? And now he lived but ten feet away from where I would spend my nights. I couldn't believe my good luck; I felt like I did back in high school when the coolest guy in the class would take a seat next to mine. Fate was obviously working overtime.

That was May; all the ensuing months run together in my memory, punctuated by scenes of near-photographic clarity. I think back on all the softball games, the late-night pizza binges, hundreds of barracks chess matches and poker tournaments, a score of movies and videos seen together. I remember how incredibly patient Rick was under Quantico's ever-hotter summer sun, after he got the crazy idea in his head that he might teach me how to catch a football and join him on the Squadron's intramural team come fall. We'd gather a few guys from their racks on a sleepy Saturday afternoon and haul their grumbling carcasses outside for a pickup game. In the huddle, Rick would sketch out the play for me, usually in the dirt, but sometimes he'd trace the outline of the route I was supposed to take on my sweaty stomach.

I was so thrilled by his touch I often forgot which way to run, and poor Rick would stand there with his hands on his hips, shaking his head sadly at the ground as his perfect spirals sailed high or wide beyond my grasp. It took me all summer to begin to get the hang of it, and even then it was only about a fifty-fifty proposition that I would ever actually catch one of those passes; Art Monk I was not.

Mercifully, I suffered a stress fracture in our very first game against those Weapons Battalion assholes, which doubtless saved us all a lot of future embarrassment. I remained Rick's ever-faithful fan, however, and rooted him on to victory from the sidelines where I stood propped up on crutches. Like any athlete, I think he craved the attention and enjoyed having his own personal cheering section.

In October of that year the Powers That Be rearranged our living quarters, giving us corporal-dudes the chance to share a room of our own. It was a natural that Rick and I would move in together, but as it turned out that extra smidgen of intimacy helped push me beyond the realm of common sense.

How do I explain what it was like to hear that soft Midwestern voice bid me good night every evening from the bunk beneath me and fall asleep listening to the steady, comforting sound of his breathing . . . to have his face be the first and last thing I saw every day . . . and, of course, to have frequent opportunities to view that fine, athlete's body moving around our room in its natural, unadorned state. (Rick was many things, but modest was not one of them.)

We were already eating most of our meals together and spending the lion's share of our off-time in each other's company. Now we were roomies as well. Was it so unlikely I'd fall in love with him?

A wiser man, certainly a more prudent man, would have found a way to keep his emotional distance, but I was, and probably will always be, a romantic fool. No, I wasn't delusional; I never fantasized I could somehow make him love me, and there was nothing in his actions that ever invited any physical advance on my part. I entertained few thoughts outside of my hope and belief that we would somehow always stay buddies, together through thick and thin, as they say. Still, as those autumn weeks went by I convinced myself that our friendship, which had by now weathered all the usual trials, was solid enough to stand the toughest test of all: my "coming out" to him. After all, a virtual legion of straight companions—civilian and military—had handled that particular revelation with varying degrees of success. I became another casualty of the nagging feeling that haunts so many gay/straight relationships, that we could never be true friends unless I was completely honest with him. Living so close to him, the pressure to reveal myself was growing stronger by the day. Gathering my courage, if not my better, unclouded judgment, I resolved to tell all. The upcoming Thanksgiving holiday, which Rick would spend with me and my parents in West Virginia, seemed to present the perfect opportunity.

Results were mixed. In fact, my announcement went over like the proverbial fart in church. Rick just sat there on the floor of my de facto bedroom—it was my parent's new house, and I'd never really lived there—looking as stunned as if I'd just smacked him hard across the face. And then, most amazing of all, this hard-bodied Marine cried like a baby.

Frankly, I'd expected anything but tears. I wouldn't have been too terribly surprised if he'd smacked me across the face. I'd have been pissed, shattered even, but not surprised.

"I—I feel like I'm losing a friend," he said, a hitch in his voice, his eyes glistening.

It was weird. Rick had rarely shown me much emotional depth; the only time he'd been half this upset was a few weeks before when the Dolphins beat his beloved Bears on *Monday Night Football,* putting an end to Chicago's hopes for a perfect season.

I was flattered, in an odd sort of way, that my news would trigger such a volatile reaction; sometimes I wonder if you can be a homosexual male and not relish melodrama, wherever and whenever you stumble upon it.

Had I simply stopped right there, well, who knows? We might have cobbled together some kind of understanding, had I deigned to give him enough time to recover from the bomb I'd dropped. But I didn't, fully stoked as I was on all of three beers. (Not all Marines are accomplished drinkers. Don't believe the hype.) Onward I charged, proceeding to explain that not only was I attracted to guys and had been all my life, but it was his particular guy-ness I was attracted to at the moment.

What was I thinking? Who the fuck knows? Taking his sudden, stunned silence for some kind of acceptance, I continued. I was on roll; I could not be stopped. I actually propositioned him then and there. I even offered him a cash bounty of sorts, if he might care to submit to, say, a quick blow job.

Rick's tears had pretty well dried up, and his sadness was eclipsed by a palpable, steely disgust. Something in his eyes snapped me out of the ill-founded fantasy I'd launched into, and I spent the next several desperate moments backing off, patching as best I could the ragged hole I'd just blown dead-center in our friendship. He waved off my apologies, and we said our good nights. Rick departed quickly to the guest bedroom. I don't know how well he slept that night; I didn't sleep at all.

The next few days were like some kind of nightmarish amusement park ride. I spent Friday night and Saturday in Washington sweating out my situation with some disbelieving friends. What were you thinking? they asked. Sunday evening I returned to a grim-faced Rick, who politely but firmly asked me to move out of our room. Now it was my turn to be stunned. I agreed limply, fighting back tears as best I could, all the while kicking myself for my stupidity. I wished somehow I could have back that half-hour the previous Thursday night.

I saw little of him as the week crawled by and heaved up finally on another Friday. I couldn't believe I'd so thoroughly fucked up everything. The only glimmer of cheer came in the form of my biweekly paycheck, and that gave me both the inspiration and financial wherewithal to try and mount a salvage operation. At lunch I stopped by his table in the chow hall—it broke my heart that he could so quickly break off our long-standing tradition and dine alone—and I offered him dinner and a movie. My way of apologizing, I said. I was surprised when he accepted quickly, seeming to give it almost no thought at all.

As it turned out the movie was tedious, and the dinner only fair, but who really cared? With hardly any effort it seemed we'd slipped comfortably back into the same old roles, as if nothing had ever happened. Heading home afterward from the Multiplex, huddled inside Rick's car as it rumbled through the Virginia countryside under an ice-cold clear December sky, we mellowed in cheap cigar smoke and a shared bottle of bad, fizzy table wine. Singing along to songs on the car stereo, I allowed myself to believe this might be the first night of many in a new, slightly redefined friendship.

It occurred to me then that Rick had driven past the exit off of Route 1 that we usually took to get back to Quantico. Before I could say anything, he'd left the second exit behind as well. Within moments the third and final exit faded in the rearview mirror, and we were halfway to Fredericksburg. Something was up, but I didn't have a clue.

Rick sighed. It sounded for all the world like an expression of resignation, but I had no idea what was up. A little bit buzzed, happy for the evening's good time, and content enough to go anywhere with him, I said nothing as our warm beds and barracks receded behind us. I was waiting for an opening, an explanation from the Skipper of our new course and heading.

As if on cue, Rick reached over and took the bottle from my hand. He swigged the last gulp of wine and shoved it under the seat with a clink.

"I had a great time tonight," I offered, his silence starting to concern me. Rick stared straight ahead at the roadway, his eyes curiously intent. A few more miles went by before he spoke again.

"Tim," he said. "I have a problem."

I waited, no clue where this might be going, though deep inside I felt the unformed stirrings of something like hope. He sighed again, then uttered three words that would forever change every-thing between us.

"I need money."

It's hard to describe the feeling that rocketed through me at that moment, a rush that seemed to start in my toes, shoot through me and out of my skull. It left me a little dizzy and laboring to breathe. I think I absorbed, rather than heard, his next sentence.

"If that offer of yours is still good, I'll take you up on it."

Even on the verge of getting the very thing I'd been dreaming of all these many months, perhaps out of some need to play it cool or at least appear in control of the situation, I said, with all the calm I could muster, "How much are we talking about?"

As if I cared. As if I wouldn't have given him my last cent at that moment.

He shook his head, as if laughing at himself. "This is going to sound so stupid." He sighed again. "Right now I have just enough cash—barely—to get home for Christmas. But I need money—for a suit."

"A suit?"

"For the Squadron Christmas Party, or else I can't go." He looked over at me, embarrassed and imploring. "And I gotta say, man, I'd really like to go."

Ah, yes, the Party—now it made sense. That would of course be the annual HMX-1 Christmas bash. At the White House, no less. I hadn't even known Rick was going, because only a hundred or so invitations had been made available by lottery to the Squadron's 600 Marine complement. I hadn't been invited, that's for sure. I can't say I would have gone if I had been; at that time the Administration and I were in philosophical disagreement on more than a few salient points.

"Actually I only need about a hundred bucks or so to get a nice-looking sport coat." He glanced over at me again, but this time a very strange smile that I'd never seen before played on his face. "So what do you think? Am I worth a hundred bucks to you?"

I was a runner in sight of the finish line after a very long race, an intrepid explorer at the doorstep to the New World—my dream was coming true. And to think I had Ronald-freakin'-Reagan to thank for it. Now it was my turn to sigh. "Yeah, I think a hundred will be just fine."

*   *   *

Not long after that, Rick swung the car around. Before I knew it, we were parked well off a little country road, way back in the trees out of sight of whatever car might pass us by. It was almost like he planned this, I thought, before my mind moved on to other, more pressing concerns.

Let me tell you, getting ready to go down on my straight best friend for the very first time was—well, intense isn't quite the right word, but it comes close. All those times I'd seen him naked hadn't prepared me for this at all. I guess I had never really dared to dream I would ever be in this situation. I was blown away by the softness of the skin stretched across his taut stomach muscles, and the feel of those incredible thighs under my nervous, probing hands. Gazing upon him, luxuriating in the warmth and sweet, almost baby-like scent that radiated from his body, I wanted to inhale and ingest this beautiful young man with whom I had fallen so deeply, so completely in love and lust.

I lowered my head slowly. His dick, hitherto indifferent to my presence, popped to attention quicker than you can say "Attention on deck!" I'd given blow jobs before—to be honest, more than I can count—but he felt so good in my mouth that I couldn't believe it had ever been like this, ever tasted this downright delicious. His breathing hitched, deepened, and his abs tightened under my fingertips. His skin seemed to grow even warmer. With manipulations both subtle and supple, I had him moaning softly in a scant few minutes. Ever so gently, his hips rose and fell in rhythm, urging me onward.

Oh, this was a gold-medal caliber performance, if I do say so myself, especially when you factor in the degree of difficulty. Judging from his movements we were making record time here, so I slowed the pace down, to draw the race out a bit. I knew full well this might be a one-shot deal; I wanted to make it last.

He came without warning, in a great upward thrust the likes of which almost knocked my head against the low-slung roof. My leg flailed out, my foot nearly flew through the glass of his rear passenger window. (Try explaining that to your auto insurance company.) His breath escaped him in a kind of a garbled yelp, which almost made me laugh. He quieted, his hard breathing trailing off gradually until he almost seemed to be sleeping.

"Wow," he said.

"You can say that again."

To his considerable credit, he showed none of the embarrassment or weird mood swings some guys do right after they shoot their load. He was actually pretty mellow, allowing me to play on, offering no objection to my gentle massages of his chest, stomach, and legs. He didn't seem to mind me asking if I could jerk myself off right then and there. He even offered me a rubber so I wouldn't have to worry about cleaning up afterward.

But it was a quiet ride back to Quantico.

*   *   *

The next day, we went to the bank, laughing and joking a little, though all references to the previous night's activities were kept oblique by a kind of unspoken mutual agreement. If he had any regrets as I peeled off five crisp new twenties into his outstretched hand, he hid them well. For the next few days I waited, walking on eggshells, braced for the inevitable moment when he would fail to show up for lunch, or turn away when he saw me coming toward him on the sidewalk.

It didn't happen. The old Rick was back, just the way he was before the grand revelation, and frankly I couldn't believe it. It seemed too good to be true. A week after our roadside tryst we headed north for a Christmas shopping expedition at a nearby mall. I helped him pick out a sport coat—he had to look spiffy for the Commander in Chief, don't you know—and in all respects it was an unremarkable trip. Until, that is, the moment he tapped me on the shoulder, and I turned to see that mysterious smile making its second appearance. Standing in the silver-and-gold glow of a tacky Nativity scene, I knew what he was going to say.

"Tim," he confided quietly, "looks like I need a little more money. Wanna take a drive?"

Tell me honestly, dear reader, in my place, what would you have done?

I wish the story had a happier ending. Oh, we had our encore performance that night, perhaps not as stellar or magic as the premiere but the notices, as they say, were good. Before we knew it, Christmas had arrived. I was off to the hills of West Virginia, and Rick was back in the bosom of his family in the Midwest, not far from Chicago.

I'm sure as you read this you can probably guess what happened—maybe you've been there, too. He came back different, cooler and aloof, with a hard look in his eye—when he looked at me at all. To all the world he appeared to be avoiding my company. One sad, dismal night in January, unable to bear his absence any longer, I went to his room, hoping to draw him out. After some initial hesitation, he laid his cards down for me: not only was our brief, physical relationship relegated to history's dustbin, but we were finished, done, friends no longer.

I'd like to tell you that I took it like a man, with a brave and stoic expression belying all the heartbreak tearing up my insides, but that would be a base and vile falsehood. Instead, there were copious tears, recriminations, even thinly veiled threats of self-destruction. I seem to remember blurting out something about throwing myself in the nearby swamp, or some such suicidal bullshit. But it was all for effect, really, an indulgence of that overdeveloped sense for melodrama.

He was gone. There was nothing I could do about it.

We didn't see much of each other after that. A transfer that I'd applied for many months previously came through, and I left HMX-1 for the Public Affairs Office across base to pursue a new career in military journalism. Covering the sports scene for the base newspaper, I crossed paths with him from time to time, but we rarely exchanged more than a few words. About a year or so after our last encounter, Rick left for an overseas rotation—Japan, I think it was. I have not seen or spoken to him since.

From time to time, even to this day, I turn to his picture among the hundreds crammed inside my photo album. I look at the stunningly handsome images of his face and body, stare into his soulful brown eyes, and I wonder about the thoughts that were playing in his head whenever my camera happened to find him—on a football or softball field, by the pool, or clowning around in the barracks. How well we grew to know each other. How little any of that mattered at the end. Ah, Rick. I loved you totally, completely. It's hard to believe you're just a memory now.

And I wonder if you ever think of me.

2

Semen in a Bullet

Scott

I first saw Hank the day he got to our unit at Fort Riley, Kansas. He was being initiated. My unit is made up of Rangers and Special Forces and infantry from the regular army. But it's basically a Ranger unit. It's not something they send just anybody to.

I was 175 pounds. Five eleven, blond, blue eyes. Very chiseled, very well defined. I was in good shape, especially after joining that unit.

I became the supply sergeant. I loved that position. It was a position of power. Everyone would come to me to get stuff.

Whenever we got new soldiers, we sent them through this initiation. Basically it was just doing push-ups, but vertically, with your feet up against the wall. Like a hand stand. The new guys would have to stay in that position for fifteen or twenty minutes, to the point where they would be crying because they were in such pain. The whole company would be standing around watching and yelling. It would be a frenzy. Like sharks on chum. They would descend on these new guys, trying to break them down, almost like basic training. They would rip people apart. They were nuts. They were Rangers.

Our unit would go out drinking together, all seventy of us. My sergeant was big on camaraderie. We fight together; we stick together. Do everything together. Usually we'd go out to a strip club. We'd all get drunk, and we'd come back together. One time in particular everybody actually fought. With fists. We weren't fighting because we hated each other; we were fighting because it was a fun thing to do. We were fighting in the parking lots, in the barracks. It was crazy. It was fun. People would get hurt, but nothing too serious.

I did really good because I ended up fighting a staff sergeant. He was a country boy. The biggest, dumbest Ranger in our unit. And I whipped him. For a couple of months that gave me even more power.

I don't think the group fighting was sexual. Although if I was fighting with Hank it could be. We used to rough around a little bit. We had great foreplay.

We used to box. We had these boxing gloves, and Hank would hit me. Like five or six times before I could even hit him once. He had a lot of speed but not a lot of wallop behind his punches. So the only way I'd be able to box him would be to put my head down, and I'd come charging in there and whack him one. I could send him across the room and end the fight with one punch, *if* I could get to him. I had to learn how to run in there and—WHACK!

So anyway, he was one of the three newbies being initiated that day. Hank was by far the one with the most endurance. You can't be the first one to give up, because that shows that you're weak and that you're not going to be able to hang. Hank was a pig-headed, wacko, wiry guy, so he was up there for quite a while. He put on a good show. But you could tell he was getting smoked.

The next time that I saw him he was in my supply room. My clerk was giving him all the Gore-Tex gear and other special stuff you get issued in that unit, things that they don't give the regular Army troops.

Hank was kneeling, adjusting something on the floor. I walked up on him from behind. I was looking at the back of his neck, the form of his butt in the BDU (Battle Dress Uniform) pants, and his high-and-tight haircut. I was like, holy shit.

Hank was about five-foot-eight, 160 pounds. He wasn't especially muscular, but he was toned. Just my type. A beautiful man. He was twenty-two. I was about the same. And he had this wonderful North Carolina drawl.

He was sweating because once again they were giving him a hard time because he was new. Right away I wanted to make things better for him. I went to the first sergeant. I told him, "Give me a couple of these new guys. I got stuff I gotta move around. I'll keep 'em busy." I made it sound like I was gonna dog them. The first sergeant was all happy about that. So he gave me Hank and one of the other guys. I don't even remember who the other guy was.

I gave him a break. I told him, man, take it easy. Don't worry about this. I'll keep you here as long as I can. He was very thankful. Both of them were. And then of course I had them do little jobs. But basically it was me just talking to Hank, finding out who he was, where he was from. So, I started to protect him immediately, and I befriended him.

One night we were getting trashed in my room. I was in a three-man room. Me, a specialist, and a PFC. The specialist was my clerk and he was already asleep. I don't remember if the PFC was there or not. We had the room cordoned off into three sections. It was pretty private. The wall lockers made it so that you couldn't see into my space.

We were pretty well lit. Hank liked to inhale aerosol cleaning stuff. He would get high from that. We would sit there and drink beer, and he would do this aerosol shit.

I had some blank greeting cards. One of them had a puppy dog on it. I can't remember what it said. Something mushy. Hank could tell that something was up. I could see that he was getting a little uneasy. I handed him the card. He asked me, "Do you want to give me this card?"

Just like that, a direct question. I was overwhelmed. I said, "Yes." He told me he was straight; he wasn't into that. I practically begged him to let me touch his face. Just let me touch him. And he did. I caressed the side of his face. He grabbed my hand. He pulled it down and put it right on his dick. He had this humongous hard on.

He never touched my dick, so sexually, it was pretty one-sided. But I didn't just give him a blow job. We made out. We were hugging and kissing. Hank's a great kisser.

The next day, he was standoffish. He didn't want to talk about it. It was like it never happened. But after a couple of days, he came to my room after PT (physical training). And it happened again.

It became a pretty regular thing. In the morning we'd go out and do our runs. We'd end up back at the unit. Hank would be all sweaty in the little gray army shorts and T-shirt. It would sexually arouse me, and I'd blow him.

Eventually he moved into my room. With me and my supply clerk Eric.

Eric was a bum. He was out of shape. He was a big dopey boy from Oregon. He had his hang-ups too. He liked to rough women up. He had fantasies about raping them. He talked to me for long hours at night about that. And he knew that I was gay. He liked to play psychoanalyst with me. I'd talk to him about being gay, and he was cool with it, and he'd talk to me about his rape shit. I wasn't too cool with that, but I dealt with it.

There was another soldier that was a friend of ours. He was from the Bronx. Little short guy. And he liked Jimi Hendrix. Hank was sitting on a bean-bag chair. I was sitting on my bed, and we were listening to this music. And all of a sudden, this other guy jumped up to get some other CD from his room. He lived right down the hallway. The second he left I dropped down on the floor and, without even asking Hank, I started blowing him. Hank was sitting on this bean-bag chair, with his hands up in the air, looking at me in disbelief. "What the hell are you doing? He's gonna be right back! He's gonna catch us!" And I was like, shut the fuck up. I went back to sucking him. He said, "You better hurry."

It had to have been under a minute. He came, pulled his pants up, and in walked the other guy. It was like this thrill that we might get caught.

Hank got an apartment. He was getting married to a German woman he'd met when he was stationed over there, before he got to Kansas.

I ended up moving in with him and his fiancée. They had a two bedroom trailer. I got one room, and they had the big room at the end. If Gerta wasn't putting out for Hank, Hank would come to me. I would either be angry as hell because she had him, or he would come in and visit me.

She wouldn't blow him.

I remember one time she was in the living room with the baby. He called me into their bedroom. He laid down on his bed, and he pulled down his pants. I was looking through the crack in the door down the hallway and there she was. I could *see* her! I was like, oh my God, I can't believe we're doing this. But did I care? Fuck no. So many times I'd been sitting in my bed thinking about him, or listening to them fucking. No, I got right down on that boy.

We never got caught in the barracks, and we never got caught by her, but we did get caught.

*   *   *

Hank and I got sent to Saudi Arabia for Operation Desert Storm.

On January 16, 1991, we were staying in Khobar Towers when the first SCUD missile that was fired into Saudi Arabia blew up approximately 500 meters from us. It was a very scary day.

For the rest of the war, we were pretty far away from the fighting. Our mission was to send out teams of six or seven soldiers behind enemy lines to report back to division headquarters on whatever they could find out about troop movements. So, because Hank and I weren't part of the crews that went on the actual missions, we were right there with the division general almost the whole time.

After we'd been over there a few months, I had my sister send a package from the States to make Hank happy. It made a lot of guys happy. I had two large bottles of mouthwash. One of them was rum and the other was vodka, with green food coloring added to make it look like Scope. We had gone at least two months without any alcohol, so it was a very welcome package. I shared it with a select few.

Somehow, the marijuana got through too. Hank liked to smoke pot. I ended up getting a good little quantity. It got a bunch of us stoned, more than once.

One of the times we left our base camp for a walk. It was probably about ten of us from the unit. And about a mile away there was a berm, a buildup of sand made for an encampment. Nobody was in it at the time. We all got stoned there, Hank included. And we drank some of the alcohol. We were all so lit that, walking back from this berm, we ended up all over the frigging desert. Picture this little gaggle of enlisted soldiers, bouncing into each other at one point, and then a few minutes later almost a quarter mile apart, then back again. Like an accordion.

Back at our encampment we were all shot. Everybody went their own way. Me and Hank were sitting on some sandbags outside our tent. Hank was so lit, he fell backwards off of the sandbag. I started touching him.

"No, no, no. I wanna go to bed."

I didn't want him to go in the tent. But he elected to go in anyway, so I followed him.

So there we were, fucked up off our gourds, walking into this GP medium tent that a staff sergeant, a specialist, and some other corporals were all sleeping in. There were probably eight to ten cots. Two of those bunks were mine and Hank's. Hank had mosquito netting over his cot.

Hank got into his bunk. I was sitting on the floor beside him, looking up at him. He'd taken off his pants and was in his underwear. I wanted him in a big way. I raised up the net and started caressing him. He grabbed my head and pushed me forcefully into him. I sort of giggled to myself, I was so fucked up. I started sucking on his dick. He got his hands around my head and forced it down my throat. But I couldn't stop giggling. All of a sudden he yelled out, "Suck my dick, bitch!"

"Shhh!" I got off his dick, whispering, "Hank, shut up!"

"Suck my dick *hard!*"

So needless to say, I climbed my happy ass right the hell out of his netting and went over to my bunk, because Hank was obviously bugging out.

Nobody ever said anything about that night to me. At least not directly. For one thing, I was not a pushover. From all the fighting and stuff, everybody knew that I was formidable. And there was the power that I had there because of my job. Everybody needed me to supply them. I was like frigging Klinger from *M*A*S*H*. I would get shit from all over the place. I had eleven cases of soda in front of every tent in my unit when other units couldn't even get one soda.

But they did make a few comments to Hank. The next day everybody was playing volleyball. Hank was sitting on the sidelines; he didn't want to play. I was off somewhere else. Somebody started dogging Hank for not playing. Then somebody else said, "No, he'd rather go play with his *boyfriend*." Everybody who was in our tent laughed. But that was pretty much the extent of it.

Like I said, from the minute I first saw Hank I was protecting him.

I don't think these guys were more tolerant because of the war. Because I think they were pretty tolerant back in the unit also. I think everybody knew. I couldn't have hid the fact that I was head-over-heels in love with Hank. Maybe the Rangers are more tolerant of that kind of thing because they bond more than other army guys. Like I said, everything in that unit was buddies. You had a buddy, and you took care of that fucking buddy. But I don't know if there was any other homosexuality in that unit.

* * *

After the war, I went back to the trailer with Hank and his wife, but only for a little while. My enlistment was up. I was getting out of the Army.

My last night in Kansas, I was lying in bed. In came Hank, unannounced and unprovoked. He told me, "This one's for you." The next thing I knew he was on top of me, making out with *me*.

He actually blew me. And fucked me. It was wonderful. It was so wonderful that it was overwhelming; I could hardly comprehend that it was happening.

By the way, Hank had to have had a nine-inch dick. It was thick. He had big nuts, too. And a beautiful tight ass.

Whenever Hank came, after he was done ejaculating, he would have like a remnant left that you could actually pull out of his dick. Like fishing line. I can't remember how long it was, but it was amazing. It was a solid piece of orgasm. It was a hardened piece of come that was fresh.

One time I put it into a 22 shell casing. I don't remember exactly why I did that. I guess it was a "I'm gonna save his come forever" thing. It dried up, but it stayed there. It stayed solid. I held onto it for quite some period of time.

−3−

Aqualung

Matt Bernstein Sycamore

It's been a *long* day, not to say that I've done anything but I'm completely drained. Last night I was at The Other Side and Gabby came in with this boy Rafael who just started screaming at me, saying *if I wanted a woman I'd have sex with a woman.* He kept yelling about loving the suburbs and being HIV-positive and Latino and that's why I didn't understand. I didn't understand. I just wanted to sit at The Other Side and get my life together. I was strung out from coke, opium, pot, and ecstasy—plus I was getting over a cold and Rafael was about the last thing I needed.

Then this morning I talked to JoAnne for two hours, she told me Chrissie's in jail in Idaho or Florida, she stole a trick's car in Seattle and took off. Then JoAnne said I don't know if I can kick, heroin takes care of me. She doesn't really have any options—there's her mother's house in Seattle where her brother beats her or Julian and Mindy and junk in San Francisco. I wanted to say come stay with me, I want her here so badly but instead I said you can come here if you know you're not gonna get strung out.

So anyway I'm walking home from the subway, glad I got this coat—it's so heavy it almost hurts my shoulders, but it comes close to keeping me warm. I step inside the house, and someone's *blasting* some awful music. I'm walking up the stairs and—what the fuck?—someone's playing "Aqualung" in my house. I can't believe it. I get to the living room and there's Chris with three of his buddies from the Coast Guard. I feel like I'm in a frat house. The Coast Guard boys are all hollering and there are beer cans everywhere. And Gabby, Seth, Robbie, and Eddie are all drinking with the straight boys like they're straight girls, Robbie says want a beer? Gross. I walk into my room, even though there's nothing in my room yet—that's what I'm supposed to do tonight, move my shit in because I'm finally done painting and I put the new carpet in and all.

This is what I get for living with a straight boy. First it was just me, Chris Marshall the seventeen-year-old-going-on-forty— tanning salon frosted hair and all; Adelaide the pothead dyke; and Gabe, the clerk at the gay bookstore, fresh from a Christian Fundamentalist family in Bel Air, Maryland. At least we were all queer. Or something. Then Chris from the Coast Guard moved in— he's Adelaide's friend. Everyone calls him Straightboy but I call him Chris, trying to respect his humanity or something. And now Seth and Robbie and Eddie are practically living here too, they might as well start paying rent.

Robbie's calling me—Miss One, you're missing the party. He disgusts me, but I go into the living room anyway. Everyone's fawning over the straight boys and what's playing now? Led Zeppelin—"gonna squeeze the lemon 'til the juice runs down my leg." One of the straight boys is doing air guitar. I thought it couldn't get any worse than the *Priscilla* soundtrack, but I guess I was wrong. I introduce myself and Robbie says aren't they all so cute? He's disgusting. Apparently the Coast Guard boys have been drinking since ten A.M. when they were painting the deck of the boat; now they're so drunk they look like they're swimming, one of them is cute I guess but whatever. His name's Calvin.

They all want me to have some beer, they're drinking Milwaukee's Best and I only drink vodka. Eddie's giggling and Seth and Gabby are chain-smoking and Robbie's perm is looking greasier than ever and he's talking about his Versace gowns of course. Like the straight boys are going to be impressed by Robbie's couture. Besides, nobody's ever seen the fucking gowns. As far as I know, Robbie's never even put on a dress, but he talks like he's the mother of the House of Versace, don't make me *reeead* you, Miss One.

I go into the living room to move my stuff. Chris stumbles in all red-faced, pats me on the back and says can you get me some coke? I say not unless we're in a club. He says can we go somewhere? I say I've gotta move my stuff, but you can head over to the Combat Zone and there will be plenty of people selling. It's kind of a joke—three smashed white straight boys looking for coke in the Combat Zone, yeah here's some fifty-dollar laxatives, sure—but BOOM like that they're all up and out the door and the music's off. Robbie starts cleaning up the cans and dumping out the ashtrays, saying oh what a me-*ss*, Miss One, then sighing like she's the richest housewife in the world, saying it's what a mother does, thick Worcester drawl and all.

I'm sitting on my futon, trying to focus, and Robbie turns on the *Priscilla* soundtrack. She's singing "Finally" and I'm about to smack her, then everyone's on my futon and I've got that smile that hurts my jaw. Seth says she needs cocktails and Robbie grunts, comes over to pinch Seth's cheeks, and says oh, my messy daughter. Eddie whines about going to the Eagle, and Robbie shakes her keys, looks at me and says, it's what a mother does. They all say meet us there, and Gabby looks me in the eyes like you betta, four kisses (luckily three sets of lips and Robbie's cheeks), and then they're off.

I'm fantasizing about car crashes and then I realize *Priscilla's* still on. I think about throwing it away, but instead I just press eject. Back to the living room and I pick up my boxes, one by one—into my room.

I put some water on for pasta and wash spinach for a salad and then I hear someone at the door—already? Sure enough, it's the straight boys falling up the stairs. I'm stirring my pasta, and it couldn't be more than a few minutes later when Calvin comes in. He's coked up for sure, looking at my pasta like it's the most

amazing thing he's ever seen. I say it's just parsley garlic fettuc-
cine. He says oh I eat a lot of pasta, you need a lot of carbs when
you're working out and I'm trying to bulk up, you know—I'll
have to try that, parsley garlic, okay.

I'm squeezing tofu over the spinach and Calvin wants to know
what that's good for. I say protein, iron, B-vitamins. He says are
you vegetarian? I say I'm vegan and then I have to explain to him
what that means. He says wow, I never thought of that, wow . . .
and is that spinach? Yeah. Wow—what a great idea, wow—and
then Chris is calling him. Chris sounds like he's about to pass
out, Calvin says okay, well I'll see you later, okay? He looks me
right in the eyes, I try not to notice how pretty his eyes are—sky
blue and glassy from the coke. I'm confused, I say sure.

I'm finishing my food and Calvin comes back downstairs, he
says Chris and Dave went to bed and do you mind if I hang with
you? I say as long as you don't distract me. Because Chris Marshall—the tanning salon queen, did you meet him? Calvin shakes
his head no, I say well he'll throw a fit if I don't get my stuff out
of the living room. Calvin says well I can help you, I mean I
don't mind. His eyes are wide and his lip is vibrating, he takes a
ball of tin foil out of his pocket and says do you have anywhere
for me to cut this?

I can feel my eyes getting wide, I get Calvin my drug mirror,
the shard from some thick old antique mirror—where'd I get it?
San Francisco? Calvin starts cutting the coke, he says you want
some? I say is it good? He says yeah it's great blow, fucking
great, and there's a lot left, we should split it. I say no, I need to
concentrate, but he's not listening. C'mon, I'll just cut you a little
line. I let him.

Calvin cuts the coke and I wash the dishes. When I'm done,
he's got two huge lines on the mirror. I say I just want a little. He
does his line and I'm not breathing. He hands me the rolled-up
dollar bill and I snort the other line, oh it BURNS I fucking love
it, my eyeballs go back into my head, lids closed and when I open

my eyes I'm high. I say you're right, that stuff is great. I can't believe it.

Calvin's looking me in the eyes again and I'm looking away. We go into the living room and everything feels slow but frantic, in twenty minutes all my shit is in my room and we're doing another line. I lean my head back and wow. We go in my room, Calvin's on the bed and I'm unpacking boxes. The phone rings and it's Seth, saying bitch it's almost one, you better get your ass down here, everyone's waiting. I say all right, just a few minutes, all right.

Calvin says what's up, I say they want me to meet them at the Eagle. He says can I come. I say it's a GAY bar. He says I don't mind, I say all right. We do some more coke and then we're off—I check my hair in the mirror, I look HOT, every strand in place. We rush out the door, Calvin's driving.

Calvin's got this tiny little red sports car and we're both wired. I lean my head back and think I shouldn't have done that coke, I shouldn't have done that coke. But then I think fuck it I might as well enjoy it and Calvin puts on "You're So Vain"—more classic rock, gross. He says is this okay, I'm nuts about Carly Simon—I'm thinking did he really just say I'm nuts? Nuts and blow. He says are you okay, I nod yes.

We get to the Eagle and there's our little youth corner in the back of the bar. Everyone's screaming for me and I'm actually happy to see them. Gabby's got his ass against the bar and he's holding Robbie and swaying; they better break up soon, gotta get that bitch out of my house. Eddie pokes me and grunts, like he always does. Seth says oh you brought the straight boy.

Calvin's the wet dream of just about everyone in the bar; preppy blond boy in jeans and a flannel, so Boston. The Eagle's all South End middle-aged guppies and then us. I get a drink and Jack the bartender looks me up and down, well I bet you've got a big dick, huh. He does that every week.

Eddie wants some of my drink of course, I grab him a cocktail from nearby and say drink this and he acts all shocked but he drinks it. Robbie's over touching Calvin's ass and giggling. Calvin's totally into it. I'm wired, Gabby says oh honey I'm messy. I say what's new? Seth's pacing the bar and some queen comes up to me, says is that Mizrahi? I say no, Dollar-a-Pound and Eddie grunts, I'm laughing and the queen doesn't know what to say. Everyone's all about class in Boston.

I get another drink and then I motion to Calvin, we head to the bathroom. He takes out the coke and some queen comes in, takes out his coke, I say can I have a bump? He scrunches up his nose at me and leaves. I finish my cocktail while Calvin gets out the coke, he says do you have a dollar. I say put it on my hand and he pours a pile on, I snort it up then lick my hand, tasty. He snorts the rest from the foil and then I lick it, his eyes are bulging. I say thanks; my hair's great, the magenta matches the stripe in my plaid pants and both the red and the magenta contrast so well with the green sweater, yum. I'm on fire tonight.

Someone opens the bathroom door, stares at my hair and says you look like a parrot. She thinks she's reading me but I love that comment, I lick my lips and say thank you honey. The guy's looking Calvin up and down. Calvin's pretending to piss, or wait he is pissing and I'm just laughing, head up against the wall, loving my rush. We go back into the bar, Calvin says what are we going to do afterwards? I say maybe Eddie can get us into the Loft.

Brian goes over to his pool buddies and I go back to the bar. Gabby's getting sad, Eddie and Seth are bored. I buy two madrasses and hand one to Seth, telling him to split it with Eddie. Their eyes light up. Gabby's swaying and here comes Robbie, sashaying down the aisle to . . . no way is it "Supermodel." Then we're all up on the runway, no one knows what to do with us, I'm pushing Robbie aside, saying you're no supermodel honey but she actually can walk—even if she is so exaggerated it's scary, she does work it.

Then the song's over and it's Crystal Waters, sure is the classics-you-never-want-to-hear-again tonight. Usually the DJ's bad, but not this bad. Gabby's still leaning against the bar, eyes shut and she's kind of noddin'—oh no. Gabby, I say, and he opens his eyes, *wha*-at. I say honey you're a mess, and he shuts his eyes again.

It's getting close to two, I ask Eddie if he can get me into the Loft and he looks at me like I'm crazy. He says it's *Friday.* Friday's straight night, but I don't care. I say *so.* He says it's scary, you'll get beat up. I say honey, it's not that scary. He says I might get in trouble. The lights are coming up and Robbie's pulling Gabby along, Seth is following. They file outside and I look for Calvin, he runs up and says you want to go to an after-hours, I say where? He says upstairs, I say sure—I'll be outside.

I go outside and it's freezing but nice, Gabby leans over to me and hugs me. Robbie says you need a ride? I say no, I guess I'm going to an after hours with Calvin. Robbie smirks and I roll my eyes, *he's* the one who got invited.

Calvin comes out with two South End tragedies: this is ———— and ————. The party is literally upstairs from the Eagle, which is funny. We go inside and it's some bougie hellhole, all sorts of hors d'oeuvres on a tray, white frilly curtains, plush department store sofas, and a bunch of scary South End gays.

I'm too wired. Calvin goes in the other room with one of the guys who brought us and I'm stuck talking to the one queen who's talking to me. I'm crashing hard, just like that, and I can't stand the idea of another drink. I try to relax but I'm just thinking why am I here, why am I here?

I pour myself a cocktail, but yuck it tastes gross. I'm having the most inane conversation, I feel like I'm going to scream so I go into the bathroom. Run hot water over my hands and sip at the cocktail and stare at myself in the mirror, I look okay but I feel worn out. Just want to lie down. I stare at myself for a while, fix my hair so it looks like feathers again, go back into the room.

Where the fuck is Calvin. I sit down and stare into space. Every-one around me is talking about this restaurant and that party and oh the shoes I got the other day at Nieman's and can you believe what happened to _____; the whole room smells like cologne. I want to scream, but instead I just sip at my empty cocktail like it's giving me life.

Where the fuck is Calvin? Some guy wants to know how I got to this party—well, they all want to know that, but one guy asks it and I say my friend Calvin who's in the other room. Someone says oh the cute one with blond hair, is that your boyfriend? I say what?—I mean no, he's not my boyfriend.

Finally the bedroom door opens and there's Calvin—he's stumbling out looking like a zombie, collapses on the sofa next to me. I say what'd you do in there and he says I don't know, I did a bump and then I didn't know where I was. I say oh you did a bump of K, and I'm kind of jealous.

Calvin rests and I'm suddenly talkative though who knows what the FUCK I'm talking about. Then Calvin's ready—FINALLY—and I'm pushing him out the door, literally—thanks—and then we're out in the cold and Calvin looks clearer. We get to Calvin's car, get in and turn on the heat 'cause I'm freezing, didn't bring my coat. Calvin's still dazed, I say are you okay to drive? He says yeah, let's just wait a minute.

Calvin says that shit's crazy, I say yeah. He says no I mean *crazy,* I nod, mmhmm. He says I didn't know where I was and the bed and the ceiling were fighting with me. I say right. He pulls the car out of the space and we're off, I shut my eyes and we start driving.

We get to my house and Calvin heads upstairs. I go with him to wash up, change into my robe. Go downstairs and there's Calvin pacing all around, Robbie's passed out on one sofa and Seth is on the other. I say what's wrong? Calvin says well Chris's door is locked and he's not getting up. I say well, you can sleep in my room. Calvin's got some stupid scared look on his face. I say on the *floor* if you want.

I go back upstairs because I forgot to put on moisturizer. Then of course I start popping zits and I'm up there forever, have to tear myself away from the mirror. I go back down to my room and there's Calvin in my bed under the covers, his clothes are on the floor. I get in bed and move to the far edge, shut my eyes. Finally.

I've got my eyes shut but I'm not really drifting off, and Calvin's kind of leaning up against me. I'm thinking I'm not going to let him get away with that shit, if he wants sex then he's going to have to ask for it. I move further over and Calvin moves closer, I pretend not to notice. Then Calvin throws his whole leg over me. I almost laugh, but instead I grab his dick.

I suck Calvin's dick, it's the size that fits right in my mouth like a bubblegum cigar, for some reason that's what I think of, not that it tastes that good just that it's small but not too small. He's moaning and he says oh fuck that's amazing, oh I've never been so hard and he's petting the back of my head and I'm rubbing his chest, he's kind of bulky—guess that's what happens when you work out. Then he pulls back and says can I suck your dick? I say sure.

Calvin pulls off my boxers and then he puts my cockhead in his mouth, tasting it, and then he tries to take my whole dick but he chokes. He's scraping my dick with his teeth and I'm grimacing, he says how am I doing? I say you need to use more spit. He tries again and this time he's doing better, I'm kind of getting into it though he definitely needs more practice.

Calvin pulls away and says can I fuck you? All the sudden, just like that. I say I'm not really in the mood. He looks confused, he says oh, do you want to fuck me? I say I'm not really into that. His eyes are bulging, he says then what are we going to do? I say there are plenty of other things to do, I grab his head and we start making out. He's doing the gentle thing with his tongue darting in and out of my mouth and I'm grabbing his dick and then the back of his neck to get his tongue in further.

Calvin tastes like something burnt—maybe it's the drugs, I don't know, but after a while he starts tasting like my toothpaste and then we both start tasting kind of gross and I'm bored. Calvin pulls away and says will you come in my mouth? I'm kind of surprised, I say you sure that's what you want? He says yeah, I want to taste you, I'm thinking he's been watching gay porn all right.

I lean back and Calvin starts sucking my dick, he's still not very good but I'm harder now so it doesn't feel so bad. I rub his head—his hair's soft and his face looks all puffy while he's sucking my dick. I can feel my dick stretching and his lips are getting tighter, he's kind of biting me and then ouch, I sit up and jerk my dick into his mouth, reach for his dick and he shoots right into my hand. I'm close now, grabbing Calvin's head and jerking my dick into his mouth and then I can feel myself coming, I pull harder on Calvin's head and then I shoot right into his mouth and lie back onto the bed.

Calvin swallows my come and looks dazed, I get up to go to the bathroom, throw on my robe and kiss him before I go into the hallway. I piss and I'm sort of smirking when I come back into the room, it's all so funny. I open my door and Calvin's leaning out the window, I say what are you doing? He says oh my God I can't believe what I just did. I wasn't drunk, I knew what I was doing, and I fucking liked it. I've wanted it for so long. Looks like he's about to jump out the window, but it's too small and I'm only on the second floor.

I'm not in the mood for Calvin's drama, I say let's just go to bed. He says fuck, you're not going to tell Chris, are you? I say don't worry about it. He says I don't know what to do. I say let's go to bed, and I lie down. Calvin's still by the window and it's freezing in my room, but okay under the blankets. After a while, Calvin gets under the blankets with me.

In the morning, he's gone, but his briefs are still in my bed. Hanes. I look inside and gross, shit stains. I think about running into the hallway with the briefs—look what somebody forgot— but whatever, I won't say anything. I don't know why, but I won't.

−4−

Uncontrolled Libe

Lewis

When I first got to boot camp, I was scared. But it turned out to be real fun. Boot camp is where I met Claudie. He knew he was bisexual. I was confused. Because I had sex with women, trying to make myself straight, all that crap. Just for my dad. Everything's for him.

He said I was staring. I could have been. He was a very nice-looking man. He had blond hair, blue eyes. Dark complexion. From the Pacific Northwest.

At first he started being like a brother. He slept on the top rack. He was taking care of me, making sure I did all my PT. He was very physically fit. I was not. I was really skinny.

He was my buddy. My best friend. We always made sure we were near each other. We always sat together at chow. Then he started doing things. Looking. Touching.

He talked about his girlfriend back home, how he missed her. He never said anything about guys until we played a little bit.

He initiated it. Everyone else was asleep. It was in the bathroom, the head. At (Naval Training Center) Orlando we had doors on our stalls, not like in Great Lakes or San Diego where they don't have stall doors. He pulled me in there and climbed up on the toilet seat. He said, "We're gonna play a little bit."

"I'm very scared of this. This is not right. This is not Christian."

...erstand; you're from a little Southern town. You've got ...daddy, and you want to make him all happy. You're the only ...n. I'll make sure you're treated right."

"Yeah, but, this is not supposed to happen. I've never done anything like this."

"Okay. If you don't want to do it, we won't do it."

But it was too late to stop.

I just couldn't believe it. I was scared. Because we had one of our company commanders get caught with one of the recruits in the head. He got kicked out. Both of them did. They were caught by the female that was the duty officer for the division that day. She was doing her nightly rounds, looking to be sure there wasn't any male-female sex going on.

We just jacked each other off. He knew that I was scared, so he didn't force anything on me. He took his time with me. We didn't have oral sex until controlled liberty. Controlled liberty is when you have all the CC's chaperoning you, making sure everything's going all right. We went to the boardwalk in Orlando with our sister company. And that's where Claudie finally talked me into it. He gave me a blow job. In a civilian head. We were both in our ice cream whites. I had a grin on my face from ear to ear. I tried to do it to him, too, but I just couldn't do it right. He told me what I did wrong. He said, "It needs to be a little bit drier." It was really wet. He said, "We've got uncontrolled liberty next week-end. We'll have a good time then."

Uncontrolled liberty was kind of weird because his family came down for it. Including his identical twin brother. I don't know if they knew about Claudie or not, but they were very friendly. Especially his brother. Touchy, touchy, feely, feely.

After our families left, we took a cab back from the airport. We got a hotel room. I got a little more experience there. But we didn't have anal sex until sub school.

Claudie helped me get through sub school, too. We studied together. We got in trouble a lot. We used to go to the mall, flirt with the big women. He would romance me. We were just happy together.

We would never say we were partners or lovers or anything.

I learned a lot from him about sex. I learned I liked to play top. He didn't like to play bottom, but he would. He said one time the only reason he did it was because he was the one who brought me out. But he really didn't bring me out. Because everything else we did was real manly. We never went to any gay place together.

Our last week at sub school, we got our orders. I got mine first. I found out I was going to San Diego. I knew we were going to have to say goodbye to each other.

He came in my room. No one else was there but me. He shut the door, locked it, and closed the blinds. "I'm so happy. Take two weeks leave. I've already put in for my leave."

"What do you mean? Where are you going?"

"San Diego."

So we drove across the country together.

In San Diego we usually got a hotel on the weekends. I had three roommates when I first got there. When his roommates weren't around we'd stay in his room. We did our best to make sure there was no way we'd get interrupted. Put chairs in front of the door. Always left the TV on, so that if we heard somebody trying to get in I could just jump over to the other bed and pretend I was just watching TV.

No one suspected.

Claudie and I are still good friends. He's the one who told me I should send in my story for this book.

5

Gate Five

Bob Serrano

Once upon a time, I was wearing bell-bottom trousers and coat of navy blue. Those recollections of boot camp are as vivid to me now as the Technicolor images on the screen of San Francisco's Warfield Theater on that July afternoon when I had four hours to kill before boarding a Navy bus to the airport. I reported at 9 a.m. and just after 1100 Hours I was inducted into the United States Navy. A chief gave several of us lunch "chits" for the nearby Fosters cafeteria on Market and instructions—nay, it was a *warning*—that we were to report back by 1700. After some quick finger counting—*thirteen, fourteen, fifteen*—our group went our separate ways, sure to return well before 5 p.m.

I was eighteen, unsure, excited, nervous, and about to begin my adventure—my life. But, before that, I thought, I would go see a movie. I left the Federal Building from the Golden Gate Avenue side and headed down to Market Street, taking a pass on Fosters. I spotted a massive marquee with big red plastic letters heralding a musical with Jimmy Cagney and Doris Day.

The Warfield, one of those truly grand Market Street movie palaces, was second only to the Fox and way above her sister-house across Market, the Telenews. The behemoth was festooned, draped, frescoed, and flaking gilt, with most of the balconies closed off. Still, it was a "first-run house." Once the lights went down, the place came alive.

Doris Day hadn't sung two numbers before another teen slid into the seat next to me. I'm here to tell you, back then, I was so fucking unaware I should have been bronzed! For sure, I wondered why this guy would choose to sit next to me when the theater was seemingly 90 percent empty. When he put his hand on my knee I froze, totally incapable of acknowledgement. I kept staring straight ahead at Doris on a swing, all the while wondering: What next? My handy seatmate seemed to know exactly what was next! By the time he had my trou open and was down wolfing on my stiff, I had pretty much lost interest in Doris. Curiously, after I popped my nut, he sat up, and apologized and bolted. I wasn't sure what had happened, but his leaving seemed to have been the last thing I wanted.

*   *   *

As both a Boot and a student in A-School, I used Gate Five as my entry and exit to Naval Training Center San Diego.

At eighteen, I was aware I had a thing for other guys, but I worked at playing it straight. It had more to do with peer pressure than any apprehensions about the Uniform Code of Military Justice. I didn't want to be caught looking at other guys.

One night before lights out on the week of our first liberty (albeit "Cinderella liberty") several of us were on the back patio shooting the shit and telling stories about what we were going to do in "Dago" (San Diego). Everyone in the company had heard the stories of how the Navy was putting saltpeter in our breakfast spuds. All that week the guys would go for the French toast instead.

With the exception of a sailor from Montana named Billy, who struck me as oddly familiar, everybody on the patio seemed to be from the Lone Star State. This one guy from Ft. Worth started in on his sexual adventures, ranging from the highly improbable to the downright supernatural. His stories somehow got us back on those rumors about saltpeter—though his hard-on was showing along the leg of his dungaree trou. (I was still looking at other guys.)

The talk turned back to gripes about chow, haircuts, and lack of money, and how things were going to change once we were out in the Fleet. Of course, none of us had a clue about what the Fleet was, let alone what went on out there.

Another Texas boy shared his sexual conquests. Evidently he began bonking women along about the time he learned to walk. I nodded knowingly and laughed nervously when I thought I was supposed to, but all the while I was certain I must have been the only guy in the whole fucking Navy who hadn't been laid. True, in high school I'd had my opportunities, sort of, but my young ass had been plagued by one misadventure after another. I had been cursed by brassiere clasps not working, my foreskin catching in my zipper, and one girl's little brother threatening to "Tell Mom!"

This guy from Odessa piped up with, "Me and my cow . . ." Everyone held their collective breaths. Those donkey stories in "TJ" (Tijuana) had been bad enough, but before anyone could say anything he went on to tell us how his cow had won him a 4-H ribbon and Merit Badge in Scouts.

At that, Billy came to life. With a broad smile, he volunteered that he too had been a Scout—an *Eagle* Scout, back home in Montana. Now it was my turn to come alive. Eagle Scout—Montana—Billy—that was it! That's where I knew him from. We had been at the same jamboree a year earlier. Neither of us had recognized the other, nor had we made the connection. Everyone in boot camp looks the same; it's like a concentration camp with plenty of chow.

That night I established that the Navy must have been using degraded saltpeter. For a few stolen moments in the "head" I fantasized about the jamboree and that big goofy, golden towhead in his Eagle Scout shorts. It would take another three weeks to learn Billy had been looking at me too, but that is another story. This is a story about getting it on in the base chapel.

*   *   *

In A-School I was billeted on the same base where I took my recruit training. Curiously enough, I was even assigned to the same barrack living space I had as a Boot.

One night, very late, I was coming off of weekend liberty. I climbed aboard a city bus at the Santa Fe Station. Besides the driver, there were only three other guys on board: two sailors and a Marine. The Marine was sacked out on the back bench seat, while a second class had staked out his spot next to the back door. I only had eyes for the seaman deuce with an ET (electronics technician) patch. I guessed he was another Schools Command swabby.

All the way back to NTC we kept checking each other out, using our dark windows as mirrors. I'm sure we were both hoping the other would get something going as soon as we offloaded. It was clear that he picked up on my interest and wasn't giving off any negative signals, but was something really going to happen?

As the bus sluggishly pulled away from the stop across the street from Gate Five, I looked both ways before making a diagonal dash to the other side of the street. The seaman followed my lead.

The stillness of the night hung over Gate Five like dark wet gauze. Security lights bathed the traffic island post and reflected off two white helmets as we approached the old stucco gate on the pedestrian side. We showed our IDs and liberty cards to the two bored guards on duty, both rated swabbies. For some reason they didn't give us any shit about our slightly illegal crossing of Rosecrans Street and waved us on through.

My original plan had been to beat feet, get my butt to the barracks, and hit the rack. I was really wiped out from my weekend.

So much for my plans. He spoke first.

"Got a cigarette?"

"I don't smoke."

He gave me a tentative half-smile and shrugged. "That's okay, neither do I!"

We made more small talk, each threading his own needle, each taking the measure of the other. All the while we kept looking over our shoulders and making sure the street was clear of observers—our insecurities working overtime.

Without words, we touched one another at the same time. He moved his head closer and grabbed my hand, guiding it below his jumper and across his fly.

Things were moving too fast. We needed to go somewhere, but where? Just then I looked up and saw the chapel steeple. In boot camp I had been assigned to a weeklong duty as a bicycle runner for the base chaplains' office. I knew the chapel wasn't locked or on the Boot Command fire watch list.

I led my new friend up the walk, trying to make sure we were not seen. I motioned for him to follow me. At the chapel door, he hesitated, then *he* led *me* into the dark interior! It really did seem he was as familiar with the place as I was. He moved to the back wall, behind the last row of numbered pews.

Little by little, darkness gave way to filtered light from large stained-glass, non-denominational, government-spec windows. We were two shadows in a place of shadows. Tentative hugs turned hungry bodies into writhing verticals. He dropped to one knee and undid my belt, tugging at the buckle while his head nuzzled my crotch. The large empty space amplified sounds. The clicking from the locking action of my brass belt-buckle sounded almost like shell casings rolling on a deck. I pulled him to his feet. His belt hung to one side of his trousers and his fly was open. Holding him by his shoulder, I guided him onto the long polished pew in the last row. Awkwardly, we pulled and pushed at our at jumpers until jumpers and T-shirts went one way, and trou and skivvies went the other, exposing our chests, midsections, and thighs.

Getting it on in a chapel pew requires great athleticism. We were both as hot as firecrackers. Once he was on his back, I pulled his trousers and regulation boxers as low as possible. My fingers traced that spot behind his balls: damp, tight, and responsive. Our faces pressed together, mouths opened. Tongues began a tentative exploration. Our hands raked each other's shoulders and backs. I felt him touch my balls. Sweat was pouring off us as he grabbed my cock, guiding it until the head was at his hole. I pushed, he pulled.

His hips moved, allowing me to go deeper, until my cock seemed to push past two separate constrictions. Moments later he gasped. His eyes seemed to roll back, and I felt his come flooding over me. Another constriction, more sweat, and his hole was as a vice around my cock. That's all it took to push me over the edge.

Our breathing became more regular. Wordlessly, we righted ourselves. We helped each other get our uniforms squared away as best we could. The chapel was getting brighter in the advancing morning light, and the space around the last pew smelled of sweat and spunk.

*   *   *

On a warm afternoon in 1999, I walked around what had once been NTC San Diego. I was still smarting over the politically motivated decision to close NTC and leave the Great Lakes facility just north of Chicago operational. One more example of beltway logic: close down the San Diego training center, located in one of the world's most benign climates, and retain a base that has a heating bill that would pay for three Estonian winters.

All around me were construction workers and private contractors. Buildings were being modified or torn down altogether. One enterprising group was hauling off palm tress, uprooting them wholesale. What is the market, I pondered, for adult palm trees?

My car was parked in the lot across from the old parade grounds, Preble Field. A dozen rookie policemen were test-driving their motorcycles. On a nearby patch of green, civilian employees were taking their lunch hour. I walked over to a World War II

5-inch-38 gun mount. I sat there, remembering the day I graduated on that same Preble Field. NTC was my first commissioned "ship" in the United States Navy. It was sad to see what she had come to.

I walked to the far end of the base, where the *USS Neversail* sits in her time-honored berth. At the grinder—an apron of blacktop familiar to every whitehat that has ever passed through NTC— I turned up toward Rosecrans and Gate Five. The streets were neglected. Many of the remaining barracks were awaiting the wrecking ball.

Almost as an afterthought, I walked up to a fenced-off, debris-filled area where once a chapel stood. Shaking my head, I turned to walk back to my car when, out of the corner of my eye, I spotted two neat rows of stacked and battered wood benches. *Church pews.*

I motioned to one of the construction workers. Without even thinking about it I knew what I had to do.

The workman dutifully trotted over to the fence to see what I wanted. He yelled to his foreman, pointing to the pews, "Are these old benches for sale? This guy wants to buy one!"

The one with the highest number, I was ready to add.

"What? Oh, those. No. Already been sold. Sorry, old timer. Looks like you're shit-out-of-luck."

6

Sir! Yes, Sir!

Aarek

Doing it in the barracks is great fun—no doubt. But it really is one of the dumbest things you can do. There's a great danger of being caught, and that is the quickest way to do in your career. Not only your own, but your partner's, too. There's a double standard, though, because chicks get fucked all the time in the barracks and hardly ever come to grief. We cocksuckers deserve equal opportunity! And while I never mess around where I live and work, there's just something about being off someplace TDY (on temporary duty).

*   *   *

I never thought I would be back here again at this dreadful naval base. It's hard for me, serving with the elite of the Army as an airborne Joe, to be surrounded by "leg" (i.e., non-airborne) jarheads and squids. Were it not for the fact that they are easier fucks than Army guys, I would be going out of my mind.

When people ask me whether I am heterosexual, homosexual, or bisexual, I tell them that I am just sexual. Most of the time, though, you could call me a submissive leather bottom. I love sucking cock, and I love getting fucked. Furthermore, I love big muscular dudes who are hairy, hung, full of testosterone, and willing to play real rough.

About a month ago, I met—and shortly thereafter fucked in the front of my pick-up—a gunny (gunnery sergeant) from the Corps. He had a nice trim body, tight little fuckin' ass, and was just as horny as I was that night. (Yeah, I know I just said I was a bottom—but the Marines have these little olive drab PT shorts that they don't wear underwear with, and they make their asses look so hot.) Since then, I'd been fantasizing about him while jerking off. Then, yesterday afternoon when I was cruising a parking lot, he drove by me. It was good to see him again, but I was torn because I was talking to a guy in the next vehicle over, Chief.

Chief is a squid on one of the local floaty-things. (Oh yeah, that's right, the Navy bitches call them ships.) I could see Chief's bulge in his Nike athletic shorts as he sat there in his jeep playing with his cock. He was getting worked up, and so was I. Then Gunny went by. Chief asked me who I was waving to. His ears perked up when I told him the deal.

Gunny parked several spots down the row. Now I was getting really worked up. Two fuckin' hot guys were just parking spaces away. I asked Chief how he'd feel about a three-way. He said that he had never done one before, but if I could get Gunny to be the third he would be willing to give it a try. "I'll see what I can do," I said.

I offered my place as a spot that we could go to. First Gunny and then Chief agreed. Neither of them worked on the base I was on. It was the weekend, and my classmates were off somewhere doing the *het* thing.

We didn't even need a porno. As soon as the door was shut and the beer was passed around, I was on my knees being the submissive bottom I love to be. Chief and Gunny were eating this up, pun intended. They had a little fuckin' airborne Army bitch on his knees giving them head. They were two senior NCOs feeling each other's hard bodies and French kissing in the barracks.

They took turns grabbing the back of my head and forcing themselves down my throat. I'm telling you, dudes, if you haven't ever had a high-and-tight haircut, get one! There's no better feeling than servicing some hung dude when he's got his rough hands on your head, and you've got freshly shaved bristles. It's the best.

Gunny laid down on the *rack* (Navy term for a fuckin' bed!) and told me to fuck him.

"Sir! Yes, Sir!"

I had no sooner got my own cock up his ass when Chief stuck his cock up my ass. Fuck, yeah! I wrapped my arm under Gunny's armpits and started goin' crazy on his ass. Chief reached over my shoulders to grab Gunny's shoulder and started the pump-fest on *my* ass. I was sweating up a storm.

They told me to get on my back and put my bitch legs up in the air.

"Sir! Yes, Sir!"

Chief still wasn't finished with me, so he continued the assault while Gunny straddled my chest. He beat my face *hard* with his cock then shoved it down my throat. This was heaven.

As soon as Chief blew his wad all over my chest, Gunny rammed his cock up my ass to get revenge on the slamming I had given him.

"Do you like that, you little fuckin' Army bitch?"

"Sir! Yes, Sir!" was all I could say.

He pounded away. Chief twisted my nipples hard with his left hand. He put lube on my cock and jerked me off hard with his right hand. He leaned over and kissed me. My legs wrapped tighter and tighter around Gunny's trim waist as I came closer and closer to coming. Finally, I started to shoot. Gunny pulled his dick out of my ass and jerked a fuckin' huge wad all over my shaved chest. Our come mixed on my abs.

The three of us laid there for about twenty minutes. We touched and kissed a lot. When our hearts stopped racing, I was ready to take a nap. Instead, we got up, went into the "head" (bathroom in Navyspeak), and showered together as best we could in one of those stall stand-up showers.

As we were getting ready to go, I checked the hallway to make sure that my classmates hadn't returned. I didn't want anybody to see two guys walking out of my room.

Gunny and Chief slipped out of the barracks and into the night. I briefly saw Gunny about two weeks later back at the park. He had his twin daughters from his messy divorce staying with him and we tried to hook up but nothing happened. After that I graduated my school and went back to where I belonged. I never saw Chief again. I hope that those two hooked up with each other again. They were both beautiful and demanding—the way I like men to be.

−7−

Don't

Alberto

Sean lived in the barracks three rooms away from me. The first time I saw him, I liked him. He was pretty nice to me and everything. The more I stared at him, the more I started liking him. More and more and more. I dreamt about this guy. I would have done anything for him. We started going everywhere together. I stopped hanging around with my gay friends. Sean had a girlfriend back in the States, but not here.

So, New Year's Eve. I had duty the next day, and I didn't want to go out. Sean had just got off duty. We were drinking in my room. Sean drank so much he threw up all over himself. I helped him take off his shoes. He took off his pants. He took off his shirt. He took off his underwear, because it was all soaked through. I gave him some boxer shorts, and he put them on. He was real drunk. All I had to do was push him, and he fell in the bed. He fell asleep or passed out or whatever. I stayed up and watched television for awhile. I started getting ready to go to bed. We have bunk beds. I was going to go on the top bed. He was on the bottom. But before I could even get into bed, just as I was about to turn off the television, he got up, came at me, and hit me.

"What's wrong?!"

"I thought you were my friend!"

He hit me on the head. I grabbed his arms.

"What are you talking about?"

"These boxer shorts ain't mine!"

"You put them on. You threw up. There's your clothes right there, look!"

He didn't want to believe it. He thought I was doing something to him. But I didn't. I wanted to, but I wouldn't take advantage of somebody that way. Not if he's drunk. He hit me again. I got mad.

"Go! Get out!"

I started throwing things at him. Glasses, TV, VCR.

He threw things back at me. We broke everything that was in that room. Finally the MPs came.

We both got 14 days extra duty, both were enrolled in CCC (Community Counseling Center) the Army's counseling thing for alcohol. The next day I went and apologized.

"Maybe I helped you more than I had to."

"I don't even remember doing this and that."

I guess he had a blackout, they call it.

"Well, you did this, and you did that! I wasn't trying to make a pass at you. I wouldn't do that. You're my friend, I like you a lot, I would do anything for you. But I wouldn't do that to you."

Unless you wanted. No, I didn't say that.

Now we're friends again, but not as close as we were. And after that, people started talking about me in the barracks.

So that's my *Night in the Barracks* story. If somebody reading this is gay and planning to come in the Army, I'd say, don't do it. You can't be yourself. You can't do what you want to do. Your sex life is going to be—what, stand in your room and beat off? I think you won't be happy. If I had to do it over again, I would have stayed a civilian.

8

Tomorrow's Man

Daniel Luckenbill

I have made fellowships—
Untold of happy lovers in old song
Bound with the bandage of the arm that drips;
Knit in the webbing of the rifle-thong

Wilfred Owen
"Apologia Pro Poemate Meo"
1917

I first saw a uniformed military man in the mid-1950s, in central Illinois. I was about ten. A friend of the family, a young man about twenty, was visiting our farm. As he stood and talked to me in my bedroom, his white Navy uniform excited me as much as the swarthy body it covered. His dark hair was short on the sides but long on top. He would take his Navy cap and catch the waves to hide them, then push the cap back to let them spill over his forehead.

Throughout school I had been studious, not athletic. I was tall and slim, but I had not developed skills in any sport. I tolerated the required high school gym class only because of the abundant naked bodies. None excited me as much as a short and stocky boy who was new to our small school. Bob Atwell had a dazzling smile which revealed an endearing gap between his front teeth. His dark-rimmed glasses gave him a pseudostudious look. Most of us in the class were juniors. He was a freshman, but he was close to our age since he had flunked some grades. I saw him in the morning in study hall. His shirttail was always out. If he sat down in a certain way or reached in his back pocket for something, I could see a glimpse of his white briefs or sometimes a thin band of smooth white skin.

Like others in this gym class—but not me—Atwell was on the football team. He was short but muscular and perfectly proportioned. After our shower, he did something no other boy did in that class. Instead of moving directly to the area where he dressed—there were no lockers—he would go, still naked, to the small bathroom to piss at one of the two urinals. He would be in my direct line of sight. I would stare at his perfect taut ass.

I began to follow him each day. I would study his body, which was like the Greek statues I was noticing in history textbooks. Atwell's cock was like those of Greek statues, too. It hung beautifully with extra skin pinched over it. This was rare. It seemed to demand pulling back.

The bathroom ritual continued for weeks. I had no clue as to why he might have been enjoying and encouraging my staring. He would never try to stop me, but finally a friend of his let him know he had crossed some boundary. He said to Atwell—not to me—"Ain't you two tired yet of queering each other?" This let me know I was not to follow him again. It was the first time I'd heard that label applied.

There were two or three others like me in the school. They coped primarily by allowing themselves to be made fun of, to be put into a niche apart from everyone else. I wanted an identity free from jeering.

For those many years I had no sex. There was only the thrill of looking through physique magazines like *Tomorrow's Man*—then difficult for a young person to find and buy. The images reminded me how unobtainable these bodies were. Some bodies were copies of these Midwest boys: photos from the Troy Saxon Studios of young men posed in g-strings in the midst of cornfields. Although they could provide photographs of boys almost as beautiful as my football player, they did not offer any explanation of why I sought them.

I had my favorites. The magazine described Luis Santiago as "a young man who almost defies description," adding that Luis was perhaps closest to the Greek ideal of any of our modern bodybuilders. I agreed. Joe Cali, "the big well-defined muscle of his deltoid is particularly noteworthy." Frank Lombardo, "handsome . . . muscular . . . tattooed." *Grecian Guild Pictorial* wrote that "the Greeks were the most artistic people who ever lived. . . . To them, the male physique at its best was among the most sublime forms of beauty." But the Grecians illustrated in this periodical had tattoos of roses, or sometimes letters spelling out "USN" or "USMC."

Physique Pictorial identified the models as sailors and Marines. I heard that my high school crush Atwell had quit school to join the Marines and was later sent to Vietnam. I looked for a tattooed version of him in the magazines.

As I was about to turn twenty-one, I had a chance to study in a University of California program in Delphi, Greece. Through various young artists and writers in Athens, I began to see how men might live together. It wasn't only the ancient Greeks who found sublime beauty in the male. I met an older artist who had been famous since the 1940s for painting Greek soldiers and sailors in and out of uniform. An early nude could have been modeled by the young man in my high school locker room. His later nudes were more earthy, with darker bodies, and longer, thicker, and darker cocks.

I had my first lover there, a young Greek artist. All men in Greece serve in the military, and he was actually in the Army, stationed in Athens. I never saw him in uniform. He said he hated the barracks and the "sweaty soldiers." I was attracted to the Greek military trade: the rough boots of the soldiers, the flowing trousers of the sailors. When my lover saw me lusting after these "sweaty" brutes in uniform, he was furious.

I liked the easy camaraderie to be found in the cheap *tavernas,* where soldiers and sailors danced together, arms about each other's strong shoulders. The sex with this trade was exciting and adventurous, involving cheap hotels in seedy parts of Athens. They would ask for small amounts of money, usually, they said, for cigarettes. My ideal Greek became these sailors who dropped their uniforms as I knelt in front of them, or as I lay naked with my white ass offered up to them. I was for the most part unaware of the desires that these men had for me. For them, my sun-bleached, sandy brown hair was blond, the opposite of themselves they desired. For me, they had the dark hair of that first sailor and the dark uncut cocks I now sought.

That student time couldn't last forever. In March 1967, I was drafted. I was sent from Southern California to Fort Lewis, Washington, where it rained every day. I struggled to do things I'd never done before: exercise, fire a rifle, fit in and not be independent. We were never alone, so the images of these young men I was presented with daily frustrated me even more. I struggled through those months, which were so in contrast to the freedom I'd had in Greece. Each night at shower time there would be rewards, but only as material for fantasies.

Once two guys were horsing around, friends of a recruit who had just bought an instant camera. They were squirting shaving foam at each other. A hot guy, a tall, blond, straight-arrow athlete who could have been a surfer was sprayed the most. Gobs of foam stuck to his shoulders, his tan chest, and even some on his cock. As he moved his hand to wipe it off his cock, the flash popped. They teased him, but he laughed. "Some load, huh?" They all cleaned up and went away, leaving behind the picture. I was about to take it when he came back. As he stared at it, I could see that the photograph made him aware of his own rare beauty. His hand slipped inside his shorts and scratched his cock.

Often, before lights out, a trainee platoon leader named Whitaker would spread his legs, plant his strong feet on the barracks floor, and stand naked at the end of the bay to bark his evening orders.

There was Neumann, my bunkmate, so naked and close to me every day. His thick uncut cock was a temptation as he dressed at the locker beside me or jumped into his bunk over me. Once he showed me a picture of friends taken in Vietnam, two handsome shirtless men posed in front of an Army jeep. The image had a strong impact on me. It wasn't like journalists' pictures of wounded and suffering GIs that had become ubiquitous by then. The photo had been taken by the GIs themselves to document a stage of their manhood, as evidence of a bond between them. For me, it was more than a photo from a war that I was against. It was my first window into a possible world of men, the other Greek ideal of friendship between fighting men, Achilles and Patroclus.

In Basic you could be tested for OCS (Officer Candidate School). I applied and was accepted into a combat branch, Artillery. First I had a rigorous AIT (Advanced Individual Training) at Fort Sill, near Lawton, Oklahoma. The program, OCS Prep, was designed to prepare you for the training to follow, to demonstrate how difficult it would be, and see how you fit in with other men and the process. I never dreamed I could do it.

We were never alone and seldom had time off. Unlike Basic, it was like living in a fraternity, something I'd never done. Most of us had taken some college in those days, and that helped us get selected for OCS. The youngest of us, Curtis Armstrong, slept across the aisle from my bunk. A chunky teenager straight out of high school, he was more like a Marine: a thick neck and strong, square chin like a bulldog. It was late spring but already hot. Curtis slept naked, his legs spread and bent with everything hanging out for all to see—especially me directly across from him. As he turned during the night, his large cock and balls moved between his thick thighs. I longed to be crushed between those strong legs.

I think Armstrong was sensitive about his age, since most of us were older. He would often strike a tough pose and convince you of its serious threat and menace. This was termed "command presence," an expression he might assume for someone under his command, to show a trainee he meant business. Then, with his chin tucked back as if standing for inspection, he would slowly break into a grin, which totally disarmed you. It was an expression that could get you to do anything for him as a fellow officer candidate. It was like flirting. This charm made me fall in love with him over and over again.

I had women friends from college and Europe who wrote me letters. They became my masks. Through AIT and OCS, I gradually built up my endurance for the PT tests that came fast and furious during the training. I was slim, and ran well for that part of the test. With the Army exercises I began to increase my endurance and built up my arms and torso.

I had no sexual experience until near the end of the training. Our lives then revolved around platoons. We saw everyone in the training battery (company level in Artillery) during the day, but there was little time to know anyone not in our platoon. Armstrong, the candidate who had slept naked in AIT, was not in mine. There were receptions to mark stages in the training and also to test how social we might be as potential officers. After one of these he agreed to go into Lawton with me. We shared a motel room. We shared a bed. It was late, and we had been drinking more than we were accustomed to. We just slept. The next morning, I woke first. The covers had trapped the warmth of our bodies as the winter sun filtered in on us. I wondered if this were a test, and if he would report back to our peers. He said nothing. He pretended sleep, but his cock was hard. My hand sought it. I jacked him off, savoring each stroke and only just daring to brush those strong thighs. He, who could bark orders like a drill sergeant, made almost no sound as he came. No words were spoken; nothing else followed. When I asked him again to spend a night, he brushed me off.

Each candidate had to give a talk. Mine was perhaps the only one whose subject was literature. I spoke about the English poet Wilfred Owen, an officer who was killed as World War I ended. I felt his poems had lessons to teach us about facing possible suffering and death. I couldn't reveal he was homosexual.

After graduation, a few of us were sent directly to Vietnam, which was unusual at that time. It had been customary for a green second lieutenant to spend a year in Germany or in a training unit to get used to being an officer. I was dropped directly into the country, into the conflict, being sent to the First Air Cavalry Division and assigned as a forward observer (FO) with an infantry company. I would be no safer, it turned out, than Marine second lieutenants, who may have had the highest casualty rate of the entire conflict.

Being part of the Artillery, I was both an insider and an outsider to the Infantry. I had to protect them with my skill in artillery fire and to prove myself in this most difficult of circumstances. I was no good at the beginning, but someone wised me up. I threw away issued equipment. I threw away the mess kit. I redid the sling on my M-16 so that I could carry it better. It was no longer for the practice range or parade ground. I threw away procedures designed for the safety of the training field and not the reality of close battle in dense jungle.

I developed crushes on several men, particularly one of the infantry platoon leaders, a 2nd Lieutenant, like me. Edwin Hansen was also a Midwest Swede and new in the country. He was only nineteen, but he had a swagger that belied his age. As soon as he knew there were no higher officers around who would care, he took off his shirt. He had a long scar down his torso, from a hunting accident which made him look like a veteran. He washed his new fatigues repeatedly so he wouldn't look like an FNG—a Fucking New Guy. In the beginning he thought that I was kind of "sissy" but later begrudgingly complimented me, saying that I had toughened up and was "good."

In hindsight, I am glad and proud to have been part of the Cav and its history. Support was terrific, although I was in two hellish operations: the relief of Khe Sanh Marine base in the spring of 1968, and, right after that, the first explorations of the A Shau Valley, which ran parallel to the border of Laos and the Ho Chi Minh Trail.

At Khe Sanh, our company was designated to be the first to reenter and to relieve the Marine base. The first kilometer out we were hit by NVA (North Vietnamese Army [troops]). Conventional artillery couldn't be used. In this battle for which no training had prepared me, I sat high atop the rim of a bomb crater. From there I could hear enough to direct choppers firing rockets into the tree line where I could see almost nothing.

For this I received a medal. This operation was a turning point in the war, the biggest story of the day, so we were hounded by reporters. One was a woman. I came across her poking a camera into the face of a wounded GI on a stretcher alongside others waiting to be airlifted out for MEDEVAC. I was shocked. She merely said, "They have such interesting faces." I nearly killed her, but restrained myself. I thought of lines from Wilfred Owen:

> Move him into the sun—
> Gently its touch awoke him once.

*   *   *

Before these operations, there were always days of waiting. We would set up near a river, where we could swim naked and bathe. There were bodies like those I desired in high school gym class. Boys with the young muscles and supple grace of farm boy athletes.

On a sandbar close to me sat one soldier making a lather over his taut body, his legs spread and dangling in the water, his dark cock hanging low and the foreskin pressed against one muscled leg. To rinse off he ducked under, then jumped up from the water. Its coolness streamed down his lithe muscles. Its movement shaped the hair at his center as his cock swung free, small drops of water glistening. He flopped back into the water, covering what excited me most. Afraid I might reveal my attraction, I kept my expression as neutral as possible. This quick scene—even as it happened—I slowed down in my mind. There the desire had to remain, it could not be transferred to caresses, movements retracing the water's brief coursing. I looked up at the river bank and saw others, still naked, drying off.

Lt. Hansen had undressed. He smiled and his hand curled around his pecs, then trailed down his smooth, muscled skin parallel to the scar tissue. His hand stopped where the scar stopped, dipped to the dark bush below, then tugged at his long white cock. He shook it back and forth to loosen the foreskin.

I never saw these infantrymen again. Hansen and I were transferred out of USARV, the American combat command, to MACV, the advisory command to the Vietnamese armed forces. We were briefly together as we waited for our orders. He let me know one evening that he knew I was gay and he wasn't interested. He said nothing else.

I saw a lot of the country as I went through various holding companies and to language school. I met and traveled with a 1st Lieutenant Ranger, Michael Lyon. Improbably, each of us had found in the PX Graham Greene's novel of the French Vietnamese war, *The Quiet American.* Mike was beguiled by the descriptions of the Vietnamese mistress's thighs: "I woke . . . and found my hand where it had always lain at night, between her legs." I was captivated by the French Colonial history and atmosphere, Saigon and the Continental Hotel.

Mike was about my age, married with children. He was also a college graduate, but thought less of his degree than of his Ranger status. I was jealous of that. I hadn't put myself through the additional rigors of jump school or Ranger training. He was serious most of the time, perhaps to give more authority to his boyish good looks. He didn't look too "strak," as we used to say. His fatigues might be bloused sloppily, for example. I think this created the rugged Ranger effect he wanted.

For some reason he called me Harry, as if renaming me would place me into his world: pragmatic, gung-ho, liking the field. Evenings were free, and we had time to drink and talk. Some days we could hitchhike to town and feel almost like tourists. We went to small Vietnamese restaurants and cursed the officers who could do this every day, who lived in actual barracks instead of on the ground as we had for months. We even hitchhiked to Saigon, a sort of daring thing to do, two lieutenants in the back of some Army construction truck. We sat on the terrace of the Continental, while our thoughts ranged back over episodes from Greene's novel.

Toward the end of our training, we were billeted in a transient BOQ (bachelor officers' quarters) in colonial stucco barracks built by the French. The rooms were large with several bunks, but only four of us slept there. One evening after we had partied, I went to the large latrine to shower. I saw Mike crouched over the toilet, naked. He was in a bad way.

"I just can't drink," he said.

So I kneeled behind him and pressed his temples. Someone had taught me that was good when you were throwing up.

"I never could play ball," he confessed to me here at this unusual moment. "My mouth tastes like a regiment of Cong just marched through and burned the rubber off their Ho Chi Minhs."

He relaxed back into me so that I had to hold and support his body. I wanted this to last, but he got to his feet. He said, "Let's take a shower. We need a shower."

I followed and saw that his cock was getting hard. He was seducing me. I thought we might do something right there, but he had other ideas. He turned off the water and grabbed his towel.

He went back and got into his bunk over mine. I followed after him, wrapping a towel around my waist.

Two other lieutenants were sleeping in the large room, but I stood at the bunk and saw he was still aroused. Mike's cock had looked big in the shower. It was bigger now as I reached and held it. He seemed to not care about the others. Neither did I.

I went down on him right there, trying not to make too much noise. But I heard small moans as my hands moved up and down his strong torso. He bent his knees and raised them and rocked them back and forth in pleasure, a signal for me to take even more of his cock and balls. I hoped that this sound and movement wouldn't give us away, but how couldn't it? I could barely see the others in the room and could only hope they were sleeping through this.

My towel was still wet, clammy as my own cock got hard. The towel slipped from my waist and I was completely naked. He thrust hard and fast. I struggled to keep him inside me and to swallow quickly. It was over all too soon. With my face still nuzzling his crotch, I let one hand trail up and down his body. I held my cock, grabbed for my towel and shot into it.

I gripped his shoulder and caressed the soft hair of his chest and belly. My hands moved as if to memorize this man's body, the first I'd touched this way in months. My fingers felt the tight muscles of his thighs. I let one hand lay between his legs, but I could tell he was now ready to sleep. I dropped into my bunk and tried to do the same.

We did this one other time.

The other lieutenants never said anything to me, but later Mike told me that one of them had asked him, "Couldn't we maybe do sex with each other?" Mike said to me, "I couldn't believe it." Whether he had simply blocked out our incidents, or whether he wanted sex with me and no other man, I'll never know.

As Mike and I parted and went to our different assignments, I reflected that I had achieved some of my goals. I was no longer an object for jeering. I was accepted by my fellow officers and was in a way even loved by one. In situations like this where you were torn apart by sudden transfers—or death—a relationship was difficult. I had found nothing permanent. Perhaps that wasn't even what I wanted.

I still had months to go in country. I would need to look, and I would want to look for tomorrow's man.

9

Monsoon

Harry Davis

During the Vietnam War, I was stationed at a U.S. Air Force search and rescue camp in northern Thailand, not far from the Mekong River border with Laos. We did not live in barracks, but rather in hutches of wood-frame construction built on raised wooden platforms, a design necessary to accommodate the flooding brought on by seasonal monsoon rains. There were six hutches organized in a rectilinear plan around an open space characterized by dirt during the dry season and mud during the rainy season. The showers were located at the far end of this space and could be reached from the hutches by walking on wooden platform bridges. Skillfully erected by a unit called Red Horse, the Air Force counterpart to the Seabees, the whole place conveyed an earthy romanticism, out in the middle of the jungle.

Within the hutches there was little privacy—never much of a concern to military planners. Space was divided into sleeping cubicles separated by panels of horizontal slats. Each cubicle had bunks for two men. Fortunately, my bunkmate, a sweating jug-head from Oklahoma, had found a better arrangement off-base with his "tee-lock," a barmaid in the local village, so he wasn't around much. Most of the time, I had the cubicle all to myself. As a bookish medic pulling duty at night, I treasured my leisure time reading during daylight hours without much intrusion from the other guys in my outfit. While the other troops were on duty, I lolled on my bunk reading pretty much whatever I could get my hands on, although I seem to recall Flaubert most of all. I basked in what privacy I could find, grateful my housing situation wasn't an open bay, or worse, a tent.

I wasn't completely alone, however. Larry and Danny, two cute Thai juveniles who functioned as scouts for the troops, swept clean the floors of the hutches and wooden platform bridges, clearing away the debris from last night's poker sessions, and removing all those offensive beer cans and cigarette butts. For a few *baht,* Larry and Danny could hustle off your duffel of dirty uniforms to the local laundry down by the river, or procure the services of a taxi, pedicab, or prostitute. These kids were simple, wide-eyed country boys, charming and always in good humor. Small in stature and nimble, their presence was betrayed only by the light thump of their bare feet as they went about their work. As if they weren't busy enough, they also cared for the unit's mascots, an annoying little monkey named Ginger—she had shocks of reddish hair protruding from her head *and* tail—and a chunky black-and-white mongrel shepherd called Jeff. Ginger and Jeff pretty much had free rein of the hutches, and that Ginger was a problem. She was always getting into things. Jeff, on the other hand, like Larry and Danny, was adorable and ever eager to please.

There was also someone else. One Sergeant Dodd.

Dodd was a tall, hairy, well-built guy—apparently one of those few men lucky enough to have simply inherited a sensational physique. He never worked out, yet he had it all: the humpy shoulders, the flat abs, the well-muscled arms and thighs, the muscular butt and fat powerful calves—everything for which people spend endless hours and good money at the gym. Like me, he worked at night, and preferred to spend leisure time around the hutches, forgoing the NCO (noncommissioned officers) club, movies, and the town's bars and whorehouses to which the other enlisted men gravitated.

There was a languorous air about this Sergeant Dodd. While he never struck me as particularly predatory, I thought from the beginning that there was something opportunistic about his hanging around all the time. As if he were encouraging a situation where something could happen. Something *would* happen, too, if he waited long enough. Biding his time—that was Sergeant Dodd.

He was also an exhibitionist. He liked to walk around the hutches nude, and not just sometimes, but most of the time. His routine didn't vary much: he'd get off duty about 8 a.m., head straight for the mess hall for breakfast, and then return to the hutch to shower. I always seemed to be around at that hour, so I was able to observe how he emerged from the showers and walked leisurely to his hutch along the platform bridges, toweling himself dry enroute. Taking his sweet old time. Way too much time. *Languorous,* as I said. He would often stop and linger while toweling his hair, which was quite short. A simple wipe or two would have done it. Instead he took long unnecessary minutes, standing with his legs planted wide apart, buck naked.

I thought this behavior terribly affected. But to what purpose? Was this seduction? It seemed only fair to give him what he wanted: an audience. But I was a shy boy in those days, self-conscious about betraying too much about myself. Sure, I looked and watched. But I pretended not to care. Not too much, anyway. Besides, he wasn't particularly well-hung.

Given the intense heat and uncomfortable humidity, it wasn't uncommon to find men relaxing in boxers, shirtless and barefooted. It made perfect sense. Sergeant Dodd, however, preferred to relax nude in a hammock, muscular legs spread apart, with the soles of his feet, dusty from the platform, propped up so they could be seen and appreciated. These feet were manly, large and wide, with big toes that curved slightly, suggesting the claws of a powerful bird of prey. With his arms behind his head, flexing his biceps, the bulges so exhibited beggared the descriptive technique of French novelists. The spread legs afforded an enticing view of his hairy butthole through the netting. *When* you dared to look. Again, I feigned a lack of interest. But the guys from Red

Horse had provided a second hammock facing Sergeant Dodd's, and I did allow myself to swing in it, positioning myself to take in the full unobstructed view of those biceps, buttocks, legs, and amazing feet.

If anyone else thought such behavior to be suggestive, erotic, queer, or whatever, nothing was ever said.

Sergeant Dodd performed his strip show for several weeks. Eventually something had to happen. It was left to our kindly NCOIC (noncommissioned officer in charge), a Master Sergeant Honeycutt, to have a little talk with Sergeant Dodd.

Honeycutt was a notch above your typical career enlisted man. For one thing, he was educated. Even if it was some obscure church-affiliated college in North Dakota, that still counted for something in my book. Furthermore, he was a likeable, modest sort, seen as approachable by his troops, yet still committed to this man's Air Force. Sergeant Honeycutt always struck me as too nice, too considerate, too smart, and too enlightened for a lifer. Still, he was a straight arrow all the way and above reproach in his thinking and methods. It seemed fitting that it was Sergeant Honeycutt who delivered the message to Sergeant Dodd. Watching the two men in serious discussion, with Honeycutt's calm demeanor and Dodd's nodding in agreement, I couldn't help but think what a compatible couple they seemed to make.

The nudie shows ceased immediately thereafter. Sergeant Dodd retreated to the privacy of his own hutch, where he lay on his bunk—naked still, I'm quite sure, spending countless hours contemplating the metal grid that held the mattress of the empty bunk above his head. As I lay with Flaubert, I could hear him tossing and turning in the hutch next door, growing ever more restless. But it was all for the best, I concluded, as the monsoons, which were due to hit any day, would have made the nude strut down the runway somewhat impractical.

The monsoons came. One afternoon rain pounded the canvas blackout curtains of my little hutch with such force that I could not sleep. At length the clatter subsided somewhat, but still I was wide awake. As I lay on my side facing the slatted wall panel that separated me from Sergeant Dodd, I detected what I thought was a slurping sound. Also, the occasional rhythmic creak of a mattress. I raised my head and turned toward the wall, resting on my elbows while I listened more carefully. Yes, it was there, most definitely, but it was not so much a slurp as it was a *lapping* sound. Again, was I sure? As if in answer, the volume rose. *Lap, lap, lap*—quite regular and unmistakable. I craned my neck, squinting between the slats to try to see what was going on next door. What I discerned was the naked body of Sergeant Dodd, supine upon the lower bunk with both hands gripping the metal grid of the overhead bunk. And both feet raised with toes pressed firmly against the metal above. And there, on their hands and knees, were Larry and Danny licking the contours of Dodd's white ass. Dodd's fist worked on his dick while the boys used their tongues to clean every square inch of that marmoreal butt. He lowered his legs and the boys worked their way down those fine muscles before reaching his gorgeous feet. The boys worked those feet with vigor, licking the soles, then burnishing each rigid splayed toe.

This spectacle seemed perfectly choreographed, with Larry and Danny playing their parts eagerly and without much direction from Dodd. Sergeant Dodd wasn't much for dirty talk, not so much as a grunt. It was like watching a silent movie. But in a moment, it was over. The boys retreated; their footfalls faded. Sergeant Dodd wiped himself with a cotton towel, turned on his side away from me, and within two minutes was sound asleep.

These activities went on for weeks as the monsoon season progressed. They became keenly anticipated by me and integral to my own sex life in the hutch. Aroused by the sensual sounds of tongues on flesh, I became a vicarious adjunct to these goings-on, jerking off joyfully to the show before falling off to sleep, satisfied and content.

In time, though, I began to worry about the potential conse-
quences of these daytime unions. I didn't care much about Dodd,
showoff and tease that he was, but I was really fearful for Larry
and Danny. The tips they earned constituted their livelihood, theirs
and that of numerous unseen relatives. And with time, Sergeant
Dodd had become more brazen. The workouts were getting longer—and noisier. I didn't want my little Thai guys to get into
trouble. Sure enough, Sergeant Honeycutt caught wind of what
was happening in the Dodd hutch and there was another heart-to-
heart talk between the two of them. Irritatingly, the conversation
was mostly incomprehensible to me because of a particularly
loud monsoon clatter that obliterated key words and inflections.
But the upshot was that Larry and Danny were banished.

Resigned to this inevitability, I returned to my French novel,
trying to find some heat in the words of Flaubert, but with many
sighs often thinking back to the lustful lapping sounds that had
emanated from the hutch next door. Flaubert came up a sorry-ass
second.

Then one afternoon, once again unable to sleep, I heard what
sounded for all the world like the return of sexual lapping next
door. But how could it be? Larry and Danny were personae non
gratae, replaced by a couple of old hags; cheerful enough they
were, but I hoped it wasn't them in Dodd's hutch. My heart leapt
as I envisioned a succession of hot scenes. Perhaps Larry and
Danny had snuck back? Or maybe another GI. Any GI! Possibly
even Sergeant Honeycutt! That would be too good to be true. I
peeked through the slits in between slats, trembling with anticipation, when what should I see? There on the bunk was the
muscular sergeant, his white naked body glistening with sweat,
legs extended upward and pushing against the overhead bunk,
hardball fist firmly wrapped around his modest dong, going at it
like no tomorrow, while that savory butthole got a workout from
good ol' Jeff the dog.

I gave up at that point and returned to my book. This was not the fantasy of my dreams. This was worse than Flaubert! Who's next? I wondered. Ginger the monkey? Well, "will wins out," I thought. Good night.

10

Good Samaritan Offers
to Share Motel Room with Sailor

Lee

I am twenty-nine years old and have been in the United States Navy for almost eleven years. For nine years and ten months I was an enlisted sailor. Now I hold the position of commissioned officer. My naval career means everything to me but so does my happiness.

I have tried to think back about how my attraction to other men came about. I don't recall ever having these feelings as a child or even while I was married.

At eighteen, I joined the United States Navy and not too long afterward found myself aboard an aircraft carrier at the Philadelphia Naval Shipyard. I moonlighted across the river in New Jersey. I worked for the Navy all day from 0700 to 1700, then raced across the bridge to my part-time job and worked until midnight. I have always looked very mature for my age, so after work I never had any trouble getting into a local nightclub called the _____ Lounge. Often I went there with females from my job. Some were married, some were not, but I found myself attracted to a lot of them. I slept with them whenever and wherever I could. This went on for about five months until I met one young lady who I settled down with. In 1991, she became my wife.

The marriage had its ups and downs, but really began to sour in 1994 after our first child was born. My wife had a lot of trouble coping as a mother. She also had other psychological problems such as postpartum depression and obsessive compulsive disorder. Though I never confirmed it, I was told by other members of her family that when she was thirteen or fourteen she had been molested by her brother and had an abortion because she was pregnant with his child.

For the longest time, even after I was married, I would lay in bed and "fuck" my mattress. Yes, even though I was married, there were times when I would jack off. I never physically handled my cock to pleasure myself. Even when my marriage was happy, I still masturbated. Jacking off gave me more pleasure than sex with my wife. In those six years, we never had intercourse more than twenty-five times. It amazes me how it was ever even possible that we had three kids.

In May 1996 my marriage fell completely apart, and my wife and I separated. The children and my ex-wife moved back in with her mom. I moved into the Army barracks at Fort Dix, New Jersey. It was at this time in my life when I began having thoughts about men. I would see these hot buff guys on the street, on the base, everywhere. I found myself beginning to fantasize about them while I masturbated.

I had a dog who meant the world to me. I called home to see if my parents would keep him until I got back on my feet at my new duty station a few years down the road. They agreed, so I jumped into my old car, loaded up the dog, and headed for Texas.

Driving those long stretches of highway gave me plenty of time to think. I thought about how hot it would be to get fucked in the back of some truck-driver's sleeper, or to get sucked off by one of those crazy fuckers who wrote love messages above the urinal. It really intrigued me. I would climb back into my car so hard that I would start rubbing myself while driving until I came inside my underwear and jeans. After coming, I would conclude that I could never perform such an act with a complete stranger or any other man, for that matter.

I had been on the road for a good twenty-four hours. I had just entered a rest area near the border of Louisiana and Texas. I was dying for some sleep. I guess it was about one o'clock in the morning. I didn't have the money to get a room and did not really want to sleep at the rest area. I just wanted to get home. I got out of my car to stretch my legs, walk the dog, and take a piss. A few people stood around outside smoking and shooting the shit. This man in his forties began talking to me. He'd noticed my license plates.

"New Jersey. Boy, you're a long way from home. Where you headed?"

We made small talk. He asked if I was in the military and went on to tell me he had been in the Army and lived a couple hours outside of Dallas with his wife and daughter. He stated he was just coming back from gambling in Louisiana and was going to get a room a few miles up the road. He asked if I wanted to go in on halves with him.

This made me uncomfortable. I told him I didn't want to stay anywhere overnight; I just wanted to get home. He told me that he was going to get a room either way, and I was more than welcome to just take a hot shower and clean up. I hesitated, mentioning that there are a lot of weirdoes in this world, many of them hanging out at rest areas. He laughed and assured me that he wasn't some killer or rapist. He was just making a courteous offer to a U.S. serviceman. I accepted his invitation. I went with him to the motel.

He let me and my dog in the room and told me that he was going to the store to get cigarettes. He told me to make myself comfortable. I thanked him. While he was gone I climbed into the shower. It crossed my mind that maybe he wanted to fuck around with me. He wasn't a bad-looking person by any means. But I told myself, no, he has a wife and daughter.

I found myself in the shower with a full hard-on. I had just rinsed the shampoo out of my hair when I turned around to see him standing behind me, naked. He said, "You are used to taking showers with all those HOT sailors." I just stood there as he began to suck my cock. I was speechless. After five minutes I came. He climbed out of the shower and dried himself off.

I tried to comprehend what had just occurred. I was stunned and thrilled at the same time. Mostly I felt guilty as hell. I wanted to get out of the shower, get my clothes on, and get the hell out of there. But first I closed the bathroom door and threw up.

I left the bathroom to get my clothes. There he was, laying on the bed naked with my dog right next to him. I still had a hard on, so I hurried to get dressed.

"Are you okay? Don't rush off. Why don't you lie down on the bed and I will give you a massage."

I didn't hesitate and did as he asked. He started talking to me, asking me again if I was okay and what was I thinking. I was trembling and told him that I was really nervous and couldn't believe what I had just done. His hands felt so good on my body that I let it continue. That is, until he tried to climb on top of me. I pushed him off.

"I can't do this."

I threw on the rest of my clothes, thanked him for the shower, and ran out the door. I tore out of the motel parking lot and did not stop driving until I reached my hometown in Texas. This experience had truly changed my life, and I was afraid of where it was heading.

I couldn't get what happened out of my mind. I thought about it constantly on my return trip to New Jersey. I must have hit every rest stop on the way—hoping to have a similar encounter? But nothing happened.

I attended Officer Indoctrination School in late 1998 and messed around with a female there. It was nothing big because it was only a one-nighter. I knew I would never see her again. I think I just wanted to get into her pants because of the challenge of her being married.

In 1999 I transferred to a new duty station. There I found the courage to venture into a male-male Internet chat room. At first I would only look and read all the profiles. One Saturday afternoon in April I decided to see what they discussed. In a matter of minutes I was bombarded with numerous IMs (Instant Messages) from various men asking me what I was into.

One IM began "Good Afternoon!!"

I replied with the same.

He asked me what I was into. Shaking behind my monitor, I wrote, "Maybe suck, fuck, a little 69."

This guy, who introduced himself as "Steve," asked if I wanted to get together.

I didn't know what to say. He gave me his number and asked if I had a picture. I told him no and before I could ask if he had one, he had already e-mailed it to me. My jaw dropped as I downloaded the image file attachment. There appeared this good-looking, husky-built redhead who was competing in some type of run. We talked for a little bit more, and he wanted to know if I could come over. I asked him if he could come to my place instead. He said no, that he was SIQ. At that moment I knew I was talking to someone in the Navy because to us squids SIQ means "Sick in Quarters." We chatted a little more. Finally I decided I would give him a call.

I have two phone lines in my house. I tried calling on my roommate's phone only to discover that Steve's phone number had anonymous call rejection. I debated whether I should go through with placing the call. I knew there was a good chance he would have Caller ID on his phone. If that were the case, calling him meant that he would obtain not only my number but my real name.

For that reason I did not bullshit him when we began to speak. I told him my real name and asked him how to get to his house.

Steve was confused because according to my profile my name was Lee. I explained that was just a cover. He gave me directions. I told him I had to shower first then I would be over. I climbed in the shower and was really hard. I kept thinking that this could really be fun or I could be walking into a deathtrap. Naval Criminal Investigative Service (NCIS) could be behind the whole thing. I sat around about twenty minutes after showering, still debating if I was going to go. Finally I jumped in my truck.

At his front door I was greeted by a wonderful-looking man with the most incredible eyes I had ever seen. He had a high-and-tight haircut and broad shoulders. He took me straight into his bedroom and told me to have a seat on his bed.

"Would you like something to drink? Water? Coke? Lemonade?"

While he was in the kitchen, I scanned his room. The walls were covered with pictures of eagles, and there was an eagle on his comforter. He had plaques and pictures of duty stations where he had been. I noticed some unopened mail on his dresser addressed to someone other than Steve. I understood that in giving me a fake name he was trying to be just as cautious as I was.

He returned with two glasses of lemonade. We talked a while. He was wearing a T-shirt and a pair of khaki shorts. I couldn't help notice his huge package.

I was getting rather antsy. I didn't know what to say. He laid back on his pillow and just looked at me. We talked about Navy stuff for a while, trying to find things to keep conversation going. The television was on so I would focus on it when I couldn't think of anything else to say. I just didn't know what to do next. Finally I said, "So, how do you usually get started with something like this?"

"I usually let the other person make the first move."

Something came over me. I leaned over and kissed him forcefully. Steve stuck his tongue in my mouth and rubbed my crotch. I was totally into it. He continued kissing me hard and worked his way down my neck. I was rock hard by this time and he knew it. He pulled off my shorts and played and bit on my cock through my underwear. I was going crazy! He pulled off my underwear and sucked and nibbled on my cock. His cock was up near my face, so I pulled off his shorts and underwear and returned the favor. I could feel the heat from his body. He was so damn hot.

He stopped briefly to take off my T-shirt. I pulled off his shirt, mimicking his every move.

I couldn't believe I had his eight-inch cock (no exaggeration!) so deep in the back of my throat. I couldn't get enough. He stopped sucking me long enough to say, "Suck that fuckin' cock." That just turned me on even more. When I stopped, he pulled my legs up in the air and began licking my asshole. I couldn't believe what was happening. Again, I followed suit and licked and sucked his asshole, but for only a short time.

Steve pulled me away and pushed me back down again to continue working on my ass while stroking his cock with his free hand. We were both drenched with sweat, and I was squirming all over the bed. "You want to get fucked?"

My eyes widened. I told him that I had never done that before and was afraid it would hurt.

"Do you want to get fucked?"

I told him no, that I wasn't ready for that. He flipped back around with his cock in my face. We sucked each other again. I couldn't take much more and told him I was going to come. We jerked each other off. I came right away, and, as soon as he saw me starting to shoot my load, he shot his. He came up and kissed me again, both our bodies drenched in sweat. I grabbed him and hugged him tightly. It was absolutely the most incredible experience. We laid there a good three hours afterwards talking, kissing, and holding each other. I had never felt more comfortable with myself than I did then.

As we laid there, I told Steve a little more about myself. "And by the way, I know your name isn't really 'Steve'."

We laughed. He said he thought I might be NCIS, and that is why he gave me his roommate's number to call and a fake name.

We also talked about how familiar we looked to each other. Finally we figured out that we had been stationed at the same command together in Philadelphia!

"Steve" and I washed up, got dressed, and kissed goodbye. We planned on meeting again. We did. As I write this, it's six months later, and we are still together in what has blossomed into a wonderful relationship.

PHOTO 1. "Packard the Sailor" in basement of historic, 100-year-old Pacific Northwest Navy town bar, 2000. (© <Seadogphoto.com>)

PHOTO 2. Bunkroom, USS *Ticonderoga,* 1944. (National Archives)

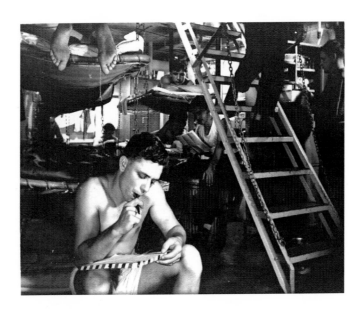

PHOTO 3. USS *Yorktown,* 1943. (National Archives)

PHOTO 4. USS *Capelin* sailor, 1943. (National Archives)

PHOTO 5. USS *Lincoln* sailor, 1999. (© <Seadogphoto.com>)

PHOTO 6. "Sex As a Weapon" author Tim Bergling, USMC, Okinawa. (Tim
Bergling)

PHOTO 7. U.S. Marine, Palm Springs, 1999.
(© <Mark V. Lynch/Latentimages.com>)

PHOTO 8. "Gate Five" author Bob Serrano (left) and buddy at Naval Training Center, San Diego. (Bob Serrano)

PHOTO 9. British navy buddies. (Bob Serrano collection)

PHOTO 10. "The U.S. Meets Australia," 1994. (Private collection)

PHOTO 11. American sailor. (© <Seadogphoto.com>)

PHOTO 12. U.S. Navy and Marine aviators. (U.S. Navy)

PHOTO 13. German aviator. (© Jon-Paul Baumer)

PHOTO 14. HMS *Ganges,* year unknown. (Private collection)

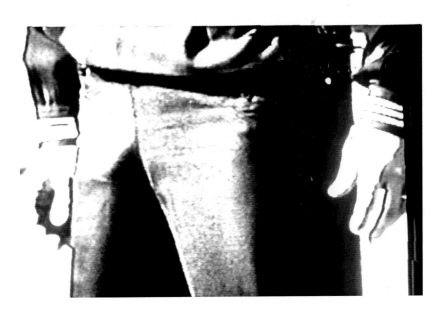

PHOTO 15. Master-at-arms, USS *Constellation,* 1994. (Private collection)

PHOTO 16. "Tomorrow's Man" author Lieutenant Dan Luckenbill, Vietnam, 1968. (Daniel Luckenbill)

PHOTO 17. Luckenbill's favorite U.S. Marine physique model, John Davidson. Davidson, too, served in Vietnam. He didn't come back. (Daniel Luckenbill collection)

PHOTO 18. U.S. Marines, Palm Springs, 1999.
(© <Mark V. Lynch/Latentimages.com>)

PHOTO 19. U.S. Marines, Palm Springs, 1999.
(© <Mark V. Lynch/Latentimages.com>)

PHOTOS 20 and 21. U.S. Marines proudly showing off to admirers at public events. (© Jerry Martz)

PHOTOS 22 and 23. (© Jerry Martz)

PHOTO 24. (© Jerry Martz)

PHOTO 25. "Kaiser." (© Bent Light)

PHOTO 26. Russian cadet. (© <Steve Kokker/maadlus@infonet.ee>)

PHOTO 27. U.S. Marine. (David Lloyd, private collection)

PHOTO 28. U.S. Marine. (David Lloyd, private collection)

PHOTO 29. U.S. Marine. (Courtesy of The Body Shoppe,
<www.tbs-thebodyshoppe.com>)

PHOTO 30. U.S. Marine. (Courtesy of The Body Shoppe, <www.tbs-thebodyshoppe.com>)

PHOTO 31. Squad bay. Marine recruit reading. (© David H. Wells/Corbis)

PHOTO 32. Bus stop. Depiction of any person in this work should not be construed as an implication of said person's sexual desires, behavior, or identity. (Alex Buchman)

−11−

The Look of Love

Danny

In 1983, I was stationed at Sembach Air Base, Germany. One morning in June, I walked into the mess hall for breakfast after a midnight shift in the supply computer room. Behind the grill was this cute airman first class cook. I had never seen him before as he had just arrived from the States.

He made me a Western omelette. I found a seat and watched him off and on while I ate it. After he caught me looking at him enough times he gave me a quizzical look. As I was getting ready to leave, he came out on break and asked if he could sit with me. His name was Bob. We made small talk for a few minutes. He went back to work, I went to my room to sleep.

I had trouble getting to sleep. I kept thinking about him. I liked Bob and his Midwestern way of talking. He was from Iowa and corn-fed. He had red hair and mustache, Irish nose, blue eyes, freckles, and a solid build. I later found out he had been a wrestler in high school. He was twenty-one years old and had been in the Air Force for two and a half years. I was a sergeant at the time and five years older than him.

I saw Bob for breakfast every morning for months. He would always sit and talk with me on break. We never spoke about anything serious. One day in August, he asked if he could come over to my room that night. I told him sure, that I would be off-duty.

At 1900 hours, Bob knocked on my barracks-room door. I had a roommate, but he lived off-base with a German girl, so I always had the room to myself. Bob was wearing civvies: tennis shoes, a blue T-shirt, and tight jeans. His white cook's uniform didn't show what I was seeing now.

I told him to have a seat. I handed him a soda from the little mini-fridge and put some music on the turntable. I found out he liked New Wave music just like I did: Spandau Ballet, Eurythmics, Culture Club, The Fixx, Human League, Nena, and Spider Murphy Gang. I played ABC's *Lexicon of Love.* We both agreed that "Look of Love" was the best song on it.

I learned a lot about Bob that night. He had grown up near the Mississippi River. He joined the Air Force to get away from Iowa and see the world. He didn't like being a cook and said he wasn't going to re-enlist. He called me "Sarge" more often than my name.

Over the months during our brief mess hall conversations I'd grown increasingly bold in dropping innuendos. Finally I even started looking over at other guys and saying things like, "That girl is really cute. I'd like to tap her." Bob was always noncommittal when I said things like that.

In my room Bob confided that he had never had sex with a man or a woman. He said, "But I know that I never want to be with a woman."

I decided that I had gotten to know him well enough to be sure he wasn't an OSI (Office of Special Investigations) plant trying to entrap me. Talking to him in my room about sex sure got me going. But I didn't want to come on too strong.

Bob said work had been rough that day because of the heat wave. That summer there were a lot of days with temperatures in the nineties, very unusual weather in Germany, a country where not that many businesses or homes have air conditioning. I worked in the computer room in supply so I was lucky enough to have it there. But it was really hot in our barracks.

Bob asked me if I could massage his neck and shoulders because he was so tense from work.

"Sure, no problem." Through his T-shirt I started kneading his muscles and could feel how knotted up with stress they were.

"That feels so good. You've got great hands." Then, "Can you close the curtains?"

When I turned back around he had taken his T-shirt off. It was a wonderful sight because his pecs and stomach were really well-built. His upper chest was smooth with light pink nipples that blended in. He had some reddish-blonde hair around his navel trailing down into his jeans. His stomach showed signs of having had a six-pack, but he said he hadn't worked out in a while.

Bob said, "Let's get more comfortable."

I had a *flokati* rug on the floor that I bought in Crete while on TDY. He laid down on his stomach and I continued the massage. I worked on his middle and lower back as I moved down. By the time I was kneeling over his butt I was hard. I was pretty sure he could feel my dick.

"Can you massage my chest?"

He turned over on his back. I was still straddling his legs and now my crotch was over his. He looked up at me and then down at my bulge. I looked and saw that his jeans were tented too. We continued to look at each other as I massaged his pecs. I could feel his nipples hard under my palms. All of a sudden Bob sat up and grabbed my neck and pulled me down to his face. He said that he wanted to kiss me and feel how it felt for two guys to kiss. He said in high school he had kissed girls, but never a guy. "I want to kiss a man, a sergeant."

He really said that.

I was surprised that he wanted to kiss. I didn't know what to think, but it was I had secretly hoped for. At first it was tentative, but then when I put my tongue in his mouth he responded. We kissed for about ten minutes, then we took off each other's clothes.

We started to kiss again, and I reached down to pull on his nipples and pinched them a little. He stopped kissing me and let out a sigh.

"I never knew my nipples were so sensitive. I never played with them before."

"We've just started. Just wait."

I had brought out other airmen and sergeants before. But all of those guys had been with women in bed. Bob was a blank page. He was a virgin, and it is so rare for a guy to admit to that.

I moved my hand to his fuzzy stomach and rubbed the hair. I kissed his neck and tongued his ears. My hand went down and took hold of his hard cock. Bob wasn't especially long, maybe six inches, but he was thick. A fire-plug dick. It was nice and sturdy in my hand. He took my cock in his hand and started stroking it.

I went down on him. I guess I surprised him because he gasped. No one had ever given him a blowjob before. He let go of my cock, put his hands on my head, and stroked my hair. I tongued and sucked for about ten minutes. "It takes me a long time to come when I jack off. I may not come. My cock is so hard, and I want to." Bob stroked himself while he stroked me. I came shortly afterward, all over his pecs.

He never did come that night.

Bob stayed for about thirty minutes after we cleaned up and got dressed. We were fully clothed and held each other, but didn't say a whole lot. When he was leaving, he smiled. "You've introduced me to something I've always wanted, but didn't know how to ask for."

Bob and I saw a lot of each other after that. We started taking the train to Frankfurt to party. I introduced him to gay bars such as No Name disco and to the saunas, which is what they call bathhouses in Europe.

On New Year's Eve, 1984, we left base and went to No Name for the party. At midnight, we kissed. Afterward we went to the sauna, and I got us a private "cabin." That night he finally lost his cherry to me.

Bob and I are still friends. We've known each other for sixteen years now. We never did have sex in the barracks again, but I'll never forget our first time together—Bob's first time doing anything with another guy. This was one of the best memories of my nine years in the Air Force.

−12−

Pissing on the Red Star

Steve Kokker

St. Petersburg, Russia—Wednesday, July 24

My St. Petersburg host Sasha hadn't learned from our drunken party with the two soldiers a few weeks earlier; Ruslan didn't want to be pawed. I had figured that Oleg, a bit dumber and sexier, might be open to advances, but there had been no opportune moment then—sloppy hugging, toasting, and male bonding was the extent of it. Sweet little Ruslan, on the other hand, seemed to know what he wanted in life, and one thing he most clearly did not have an appetite for was to be fondled insistently by a letch like Sasha. Yet the massages and caresses started up again tonight. Ruslan shifted to another seat and repeated, "Sasha, *vsyo, vsyo!*" Enough! They exchanged words I couldn't catch. When it was apparent that nothing was going to happen, Sasha nodded off to sleep. Ruslan and I took our cues and slipped out onto the streets, already bright as midday by 5 a.m.

Ruslan at first seemed agitated and kept looking down, frowning. He started talking very fast, but my rudimentary knowledge of Russian could only decipher "But I told him I like *girls!* I told him to *stop!*" I managed to ask if he'd ever been interested in men—no, he's never tried it, never wanted to, doesn't now. I told him that Sasha wasn't the only one attracted to him, but that I didn't want what he didn't want. He looked over and draped his arm around my shoulder, smiling, hugging me close for an instant. He changed the subject after that and was back to his cheery self, chatting about other things. He absolutely had to be back at the base by 6 a.m. or his absence would be discovered.

"Trouble, big trouble," he smiled, rolling his eyes and pulling at his Metallica T-shirt.

Hours earlier, he'd ducked into a darkened alleyway to change from his uniform to his civvies to go wandering with me all night, but he couldn't be seen in heavy metal gear by his commanders. I flagged down a cab and jumped in with him.

At the base, in the city center near the main post office, we walked up to dark green steel gates with red stars freshly painted on them. Ruslan looked at me with those eyes of his, sad as a trumpet player's, puffy because of the hour. Then, with a mischievous grin, he said in English, "Stiiv, Stiiv, you come," tilting his head toward the gates. I looked at him dumbly.

"You don't want to?" he teased. "You not interested?"

"Of course," I told him, "but, er, trouble? Commander? Bang bang?" A friend had told me of other foreign soldier admirers whose giddily lustful incursions onto military zones had climaxed in detection, detainment, and expulsion from the Russian Federation.

Ruslan rolled his eyes as if I were being absurd and started banging on the metal gates to summon whoever was supposed to be guarding them. A sleepy-eyed soldier appeared through the space between the doors on the other side of the gates. Ruslan barked something out and the heavy door was pushed creakily open. He took my arm and led me inside. The gatekeeper shuffled off without giving me a second look.

Ruslan led me to what looked like some kind of waiting area, or hang-out space, on raised ground overlooking a ratty jungle-gym with suspended tires and poles and rusted parallel bars. "Wait here." He left me by three wooden benches. I was alone.

At the stroke of six a bugle bleated, somewhere in the distance a tinny radio was switched on, and the base began to stir. I had a good overview of the courtyards. A group of soldiers spilled out of one door, stood at attention, and commenced running in circles. Over to the left a soldier opened a garage door, and a jeep engine chugged to life. I looked back at the guard post, but the gatekeeper was still sitting slouched in his chair.

I tried to take everything in, but worried that I was probably as visible to some unseen commander as all his little troops were to me.

At last, Ruslan returned, in uniform.

"Stiiv."

He told me to follow him, to take a look around, to take pictures of anything I wanted to. "No problem," he kept repeating, amused at my trepidation. He led me behind a building to see the guard dogs. They were locked up behind a disconcertingly rickety fence, up to which two soldiers suddenly strode, and onto which they together enjoyed their morning piss.

The one German shepherd and the one Doberman started barking furiously when they saw us approach, fixing their gaze particularly intently on me, the man with no uniform. In the cinema playing out in my mind, watching the action from above, the camera cut to the stern commander, peering down critically from his aerie, eyes opening wider as he espied me in my jeans and sweatshirt, my Olympus in hand as if it were my only protection. But Ruslan calmed the dogs down, and we were soon both petting them through the fence. The German shepherd was even let out to pose for a photo with me and gave me a shy, ingratiating lick.

"You want to see where we sleep?" asked Ruslan. Again with that sweet grin. He knew it was a stupid question. We walked back around the building. As we ducked into a dark doorway and started up the concrete stairs, squeezing past a stream of first-year cadets running down for their morning work-out, I did my best to look nonchalant.

At the top of the stairs, another half-dozen flew past me, pulling their jackets on, tying their belts up. A narrow doorway opened onto an enormous open squad room housing some 200 soldiers, crammed into semi–partitioned clusters of bunks and single beds pushed together. I followed Ruslan, my head swiveling around, trying to take it all in. It had been at least twenty minutes since reveille, but about half of the guys were still hanging around. Some of them were still sleeping, others standing and stretching, some pulling on their shirts, some scratching their heads or tummies, others already dressed and lighting cigarettes. Some were at the sinks brushing their teeth, and still others were downstairs in the shower room and toilet, which Ruslan had assumed I wasn't interested in seeing (his only major miscalculation of the day).

Ruslan was enjoying playing host, presenting me with something he knew was for me exotic. If I had held power in our previous meetings through my financial ability to provide us with a good time, or by my perceived superiority due merely to my place of birth, then here he was able to tip the scales in his favor. He was showing me off, his foreigner. He encouraged me to keep taking photos, and called his pals over to pose for me, or to snap a shot of me in his entourage.

A few guys stared at me, but no one paid particular attention, and I stopped worrying about being caught once I realized that, at least at that hour, the battalion was seemingly self-run by soldiers.

There was one photo I did not take, of two soldiers lying side-by-side in adjacent single beds that had been pushed together. They were asleep, lying with their heads angled and touching, white sheets tucked under their chins. I can see the dark-haired boy's flushed cheeks even now. I was too shy to stop and focus on that moment, which I knew to be dully ordinary to everyone around me, lest my focusing might obviously transform it into something else. Like someone shouting "Fag!" in a shower-room. Yet, while I regret that missed, priceless shot, the scene remains more vibrant and clear in my memory than most any of my thousands of photos.

Back downstairs, I worked up the nerve to ask Ruslan where the toilets were. I really did have to go, but also wanted to live out this fantasy to the fullest and imagined sauntering up to a *pissoir* alongside a sweet soldier with morning breath and casually uttering the Russian equivalent of "What's up?"

"Minimal ili maximal?" he asked me.

Minimal. He led me back downstairs, disappointingly past the soldiers' toilets, and once outside, despite my protests that I didn't mind using a smelly washroom, he pointed toward one of the garage's large open, metal doors. I was to piss against this, fully visible to anyone in the courtyard facing it. I scrunched my forehead into a questioning frown.

"Yes, yes. No problem!"

I headed toward the door as if it were my daily destination, unzipped myself confidently and stood, waiting.

Nothing. Military trucks and jeeps revved up around me. No time to be pee shy! I thought of Christmas for a moment and let go, watched all the while by a sleepy soldier, one eye shut, sitting in the driver's seat of a jeep parked outside the garage. I pondered the cultural meaning of a foreigner, illegally on a Russian military base, pissing on it, marking territory. The only way I could connect with this world? As I shook the droplets off more than I needed to, I gulped as I saw Ruslan approaching me in the company of his pal.

Oleg was as sexy as I recalled, maybe more so. Sleepy eyes, crooked smile, ill-fitting uniform. I was happy to see him. He was surprised to see me. We slapped hands together. But my night in the barracks was just about over.

Ruslan, almost motherly in his handling of me, had seen to it that I'd be officially escorted home. The three of us stood by the gates, waiting, making plans to meet up again. Soon, a jeep screeched to a halt in front of us. The gates were opened, Ruslan gave me a quick, hard hug, Oleg slapped hands with me once more then someone pushed me into the back seat and the jeep went tearing like a race car out into the quiet, early-morning civilian street. The two in front said nothing. I wondered what they were thinking of my visit, if anything.

*   *   *

Saturday, July 27

Ruslan was late but worth the wait, especially because in tow with him was Oleg. Once again, I was struck by just how much more than Ruslan, Oleg played at being macho. What made his tough-boy stance all the more attractive to me was my strong sense that, at heart, he was a real softie.

I bought us all some alcohol and something to eat, and we went promenading along the Neva river. Ruslan wanted to get someone to take a photo of the three of us, and Oleg immediately seized this as an opportunity to meet chicks.

He was a kid, I saw, a boy playing a man. We boringly stood around waiting for a pretty girl to pass by. Even Ruslan grew annoyed.

"What's the difference if she's pretty or not?" he demanded. "We only want her to take a picture!"

But for Oleg, of course, the difference was great. Finally, after Ruslan grew so exasperated that he was reduced to shouting expletives, Oleg asked a shy-looking, not terribly attractive young women to do the deed. She was clearly not interested in further discussion, and started walking away before the flash had even faded. But that didn't stop Oleg from later talking about how pretty she was . . . wasn't she?

We kept walking, and ended up back in the city looking for a store that was open—it was time for me to fork out for more goodies. I didn't mind. It was understood. And we were having fun. But near the store, Oleg started talking to a group of four drunken and not terribly civilized-looking girls, two of whom were sporting those frighteningly phosphorescent piss-yellow sweaters so popular here this summer. This added company didn't appeal to me or Ruslan too much, but it seemed that they were there to stay; they had been out on the hunt too, just as Oleg pretended to be.

Yet just as soon as he'd "caught" them, Oleg proceeded to ignore them and became more attentive to me than he'd been all evening, walking ever closer to me, and whispering in my ear that the girls were really *"cauchemars"* (like in French: nightmares!). Ruslan, ever the gentleman, grudgingly took up the conversation Oleg had abruptly cut off to chum up to me. I suddenly grew more tolerant of the girls' company. As we all walked back toward the Neva along ulitsa Gorokhovaya, Ruslan and the girls behind us, I looked at Oleg .

* * *

Here was that shy spark of interest I usually choose to disbelieve in others. Experienced as I am with male game-playing, I had let myself become quickly convinced that Oleg's girl-hunting was to the bone. I go to lengths to assume that the straight men I fancy cannot possibly be interested in male sexual contact, and even if so, certainly not with me. This attitude solidifies my straight-male fantasy and shelters me from both possible rejection and probable action.

The group of us settled on a bench on the embankment, across from the bushes where the naval cadets from the nearby academy go to piss. It was to be our home for the rest of the night. Sitting down, we attended to our spoils—vodka, juice (I was thinking of myself—I still needed to dilute the hellfire these guys were happy to pour straight down their throats), sausages, and, of course, cigarettes. Drinks were poured first, and downed quickly. A second round followed immediately, in keeping with one of Russia's most popular sayings: "Between the first and second, the pause is not long." (It rhymes in Russian.)

Oleg made sure to sit next to me and drape an arm sloppily around my shoulders, leaning deep into my neck to tell me drunken nonsense. Most of it was in a slurred Russian I didn't understand, but it was the kind of talk that included: "Whoa, vodka good!", "Canada good country!", "Russian vodka good!", and "You my good friend!" Egged on by my own equally effusive responses, these exclamations mounted to a feverish pitch, drawing us physically ever closer, until our cheeks were brushing.

The most outspoken of the girls was the blonde one, Nadia. I grew to like her despite her sickly yellow sweater glaring brighter than a Parisian car's headlights. She kept trying to maneuver herself next to me on the bench. Spunky, bold, and confident, she asked me every intelligent question she could think up about Canada and made it clear that she was interested in meeting up with me again.

Oleg, however, intercepted her obvious plays for me and always made sure to be sitting next to me. *"Nyet!"* he shouted at her once as they simultaneously both targeted the seat to my right, their rival rumps poised in hover above the bench and colliding in a brief struggle. Oleg won. Straightening up, Nadia, hands on her defeated hips, glared at him.

"I have to talk to him!" he said, in a slightly softer tone, but confident that she would be forced to concede that guy talk naturally takes precedence over anything "a girl" might have to say to me.

"Just for a few minutes," I offered, not sounding as apologetic as I tried to. Nadia went off in a huff, promising to be back.

Oleg wrapped his arms tightly around me, lifting me up, trying to carry me, bride-over-the-threshold style. Didn't much succeed, but I escaped unscathed. Pushing me back down onto the bench he, undaunted, proceeded to engage me in an arm-wrestling bout, yelling out, "Stiiv, no! Stiiv, no!" to my "Yes! Yes!" I was winning. He twisted my arm toward him in such a way that my face was pressed into the old Slavic block letters spelling out his family name on the patch sewn into the fiber above his breast pocket. I looked up to meet his eyes. We kept exerting pressure, gripping each other's hands tighter. His exclamations were directed straight into my face, bits of spittle spraying my forehead and cheeks, encouraging me to respond in kind, my mouth dangerously close to his.

A cloudy look passed across Oleg's face. He made an effort to stand up and with some difficulty walked the few feet to a nearby tree, behind the bench. He fumbled for his fly. I followed him there, no one seeming to notice, and asked if he needed help. It wasn't as tacky as it sounds, for he truly seemed like he needed some. He stared blankly at me as a first dribble of pee escaped from his fly. He had hardly got his penis out, and it poked, foreskin unretracted, sideways through the too-small opening he'd made, splattering out piss half onto the tree, half down his pant leg. I told him to be careful, and made some abortive effort to pull his penis out properly for him, but he just stared at me as if he were trying to understand what I was saying to him, even as he continued to effectively piss his pants. Oleg's drinking was clearly something he had no control over.

Oleg staggered back to the bench and fumbled in his bag. Ruslan gave him his own uniform pants when he figured out what had happened. Awkwardly, Oleg peeled off his soggy trousers and slipped on the khaki camouflage ones in silence, with me holding his shoulders to balance him. I found this spectacle somewhat disturbing, but exciting.

As we were about to return to our places on the bench, Nadia reappeared with a determined look. As drunk as he was, seeing her approach, Oleg sprung to life and again muscled her out to sit squash against my right side. The three of us laughed. But this time she wasn't going to be dismissed so easily and with disarming élan she took her seat right on my left knee. She faced the other way, but every so often would turn around and ask me something, like "Have you been to the Hermitage yet?"

Oleg and I meanwhile resumed our conversation.

"Stiiv! Russia good country?"

"Very good!"

We repeated our old themes with even greater intensity than before, if perhaps also a bit more sloppily. His arm was around my shoulder now. I slipped my arm behind his back, grabbed his pant thighs and pulled him to me. Our cheeks pressed together again.

"Very good country!"

He started to mutter a string of words, meaningless, incomprehensible, and I knew, even in my vodka haze, that this was the time. I turned to face him and—our lips met. And stayed clenched.

I seized for a moment, but closed my eyes automatically. Racing through my mind: "so soft and wet." I pressed my lips deeper into his and felt, for an instant, his tongue.

Of course we pulled apart—he did—and he continued muttering, as if the kiss has been part of one long sentence, a wayward accent. I looked around to see if anyone had been looking. All I saw was yellow neon. Nadia's radioactive sweater was effectively blocking Oleg and I from the others' view.

I had imbibed sufficient alcohol, but not enough *not* to think to myself: I can't believe this is happening.

I turned back and tried to pick up on his words. Something about Montreal. He wasn't making sense but couldn't stop talking, and so I just leaned forward and kissed him. This time he more insistently, more consciously pushed into me, opening and closing his mouth against mine, and slipped his tongue inside me with a few quick flicks. So wet, the tongue of a hungry soldier. He pulled back again, giving his head a little shake.

I looked to my left. Neon. No one had seen anything.

After yet another group reshuffle (these were usually initiated by Ruslan's frequent trips across the street to pee in the bushes—he was too shy to use the tree behind us), Nadia was standing up with another girl, and Oleg was still pressed up against me, telling me in a soft, gentle, suddenly quite distinct, even articulate voice about his hometown of Tula. His affectionate manner, his amiability, and the way he had of looking at me sideways, his sexy, slit eyes now puffy. . . . It all felt so—natural. Even as fired up as I was, I just tried to enjoy this intimacy. After a final note about the samovars I must come to Tula to buy when he gets out of the army, he let out a wide yawn and curled down onto my lap, settling into my crotch as a pillow, smiling. I automatically placed my hand underneath his shirt and started squeezing his neck, back, shoulders.

"Whoa, yes! Massage, whoa . . . good!"

I continued, letting my fingers run slowly and thoughtfully down his back, kneading his flesh. My erection was pressing through my pants into his cheek. He didn't seem to mind. Making himself even more comfortable, he managed to bring his legs up onto the bench, in the process inadvertently, sharply kicking one of the girls, making her jump up and howl with indignation. Oleg nestled even deeper into me, curling his arm under his chin and closing his eyes, mumbling softly, sleepily, a little boy who has just been tucked in by his mommy.

He dozed off. Then he started to shiver. His lips trembled, his cheek quivered. His arms contracted from the cold. St. Petersburg's "white nights" are fragile and cool beauties. By the River Neva, throughout the summer, the breeze always cuts through a layer or three of clothes, no matter how hot the day before has been. Drunk and fatigued, Oleg had little resistance to the chills. I rubbed his shoulders some more, then hugged him closer to my body, transferring my warmth.

I sat stroking his hair, caressing his cheeks, and gently squeezing his shoulders as he drifted off into a half-sleep. When he started shivering more violently, his curled body shaking in my arms, I took off my jacket and lay it over him. My first thought was to keep him warm, but then it occurred to me that my jacket would also conceal my hands from view.

My hand snaked under the jacket, around Oleg's thighs and over to his crotch. Looking around to make sure no one was noticing, hoping that my own (moderate) level of inebriation wasn't dulling my normally sharp (excessive) sense of caution, I felt for the buttons of his camouflage pants. With my thumb and forefinger, I managed to unsnap one of them. My finger found his cock, which was half squished between his legs, and massaged it lovingly.

Of course I felt like a perv, half recalling stock film images of lecherous men who take advantage of drunken youths. But a number of justifications sprung to my defense:

- It was clear that Oleg was not unresponsive to a certain erotic interplay, and this was quite in keeping to the buildup of our intimacy over the evening.
- If he was aware of what I was doing and didn't like it, he could make some shifting motions or grunts in the negative.
- If he was unaware, then he'd never remember anyway.
- It was satisfying for me at least some of the erotic promises accorded me that night.

Our little crowd was dispersing. It was well past 5 a.m. and already quite bright. Nadia pressed her phone number into my free hand and walked to the corner with her friends. Ruslan kneeled in front of us and with great seriousness implored that we had to get going.

"Time, time."

We made our first attempts to rouse Oleg, who was by now sound asleep on my lap. I pushed, Ruslan pulled; gently he slapped his buddy's face.

"Oleg! *Davai!*"

Ruslan persisted until at length he elicited some sign of life from Oleg, who, now leaning against my shoulder, with utmost reluctance opened his bleary eyes to the world before him. We maeuvered him to an upright position. With all his might he kept leaning back against me and repeatedly tried to curl back up into my lap. We restrained him until it seemed I had a firm grip on him. Ruslan walked toward the street and tried to flag down a cab. One stopped, but as soon as the driver saw Oleg he sped off.

I held Oleg tight, trying to keep him steady. He was back to muttering soft syllables to me I couldn't understand. He leaned into me and rested his head against my chest. I bent down and kissed his neck.

Finally, Ruslan found a cab, and we lifted/carried Oleg to it, pushing him into the back seat. I sat in front. We took off. When I looked back, I saw Oleg's head bobbing puppet-like with the potholes. His eyes were wide open but not registering much, fixed and disturbingly intent on me.

Back at the entrance to the base, I paid for the overpriced ride and helped Ruslan struggle to drag his drunken comrade's meaty frame toward the gate. As soon as Ruslan turned to close the cab door, Oleg wrapped his arms around me, leaning all his weight onto me. He squeezed me tight and let out what I can only describe as a growl. Though Ruslan seemed in a hurry to end this spectacle, there was nothing much he could do to pull his friend free from this bear hug.

Finally, I unclenched us and, with Ruslan, carried Oleg up to those gates. Yet as soon as Ruslan let go his grip to bang on the metal gates, Oleg once again turned to me and embraced me with all his might.

"Stiiv! Where are you going?" he pleaded, seemingly close to bursting into tears. *"What is it?"*

I squeezed him tight against me and suddenly felt a bit tragic. As Ruslan continued banging and yelling for someone to open the gates. I kissed Oleg's neck some more. This was about to end, I thought.

"Stiiv!"

The doors clanged open, and my heart sank with the sound. Ruslan maneuvered us as a unit toward the entrance to the base. I helped pass Oleg across the threshold, to Ruslan and some other soldier.

When Oleg was wrested from my grip, he looked at me and said something with my name in it. It sounded more serious, more urgent than any of his previous mutterings. I glanced at this second soldier for his reaction but he just rolled his eyes as if to say, "He's wasted!" Ruslan's face was inscrutable. The soldiers each grabbed an arm and carried/dragged Oleg off, backward.

Oleg continued staring right into my eyes until the steel doors banged shut in front of me. Involuntarily I pressed forward and peered through a slit until he disappeared down the courtyard. It's a sight I won't forget.

I have since often wondered what it was exactly that Oleg said.

Barracks Gang Bang

Gayle Martin

My entire body hurts. Even though it hurts when I laugh, I can't help chuckling when I think that for several hours last night I actually thought the evening was going to be a complete washout.

I got to the Rusty Spur around 10:30 p.m. after an hour-and-a-half drive from L.A. People tell me I'm crazy for making such a drive, but the only thing truly crazy about it is the extraordinary anticipation I feel on the way there. The excitement starts to mount as I pass the first entrance to Camp Pendleton at San Onofre. Twenty minutes later, when I exit the freeway and come around the curve to pass the "Welcome to Oceanside" sign, my heart beats even faster and my mouth goes dry. One, two, three lights to the right-hand turn on Pier View Way and then a slow cruise past the bar to see what's hanging around outside.

Once inside I find room for myself at the middle of the bar, order a Corona and turn in my seat—one leg hooked over the chair-back—to scan the action at the pool tables and in the darker corners of this dive. Some Marines I know refer to it sneeringly as The Crusty Spur. But its retro seediness is one reason why I like it. No one's dressed to impress or self-consciously posing. Best of all, there is little in the way of competition. I get to take my pick of all those homesick cowboys and southerners shouting out the words to their favorite country songs. Of course, this means that I am forced to listen to country music myself, but I consider it a small price to pay for being able to pick from such an excellent crop.

Last night, not long after my arrival, I noticed this really tall hunky Marine who was big all over. We started talking. He was a staff sergeant. Even better. He introduced me to a buddy of his who was also a staff sergeant, and cute. Even better! Did I actually believe they were staff sergeants? No, not for a second. They were both too young. I said as much, but they stuck to their story, so I let it go. (Ultimately, I don't care what rank they are as long as they really are Marines. I've even screwed privates.) We chatted for a bit until the big one abruptly upped and moved down to the other end of the bar to talk to these two other women who are in there all the time. I couldn't fucking believe it. They are absolute hags and much older than I am. Both must be in their forties, trowel on the makeup, and must wish that they had heard of UV protection before their faces turned to Naugahyde. I was absolutely livid, and it just put me off the whole night. What made it all the worse, though, was that I had a tough time hiding my feelings. This Marine knew that I was irritated and that he was the reason I was so put out. Of course he was quite pleased by that knowledge. Occasionally he threw me these utterly insincere, toothy snarling grins from across the room, which just set me on a slow burn.

Though I kept looking around, it really didn't seem as though there was anyone there who had potential. There was one attractive blond Marine playing pool who was just my type, but one quick glance into his eyes told me he was totally drunk. As a result of a certain recent experience, I was determined to stay clear since I actually wanted to get laid tonight, not just fuss around with a half-erect dick.

There were three young guys near me, but I usually look for a loner because it is difficult to peel one Marine away from the pack. However, two of these guys were particularly cute, one a clearly Irish blue-eyed blond (my favorite type) and the other dark-haired. Both of them had the build that I like: BIG. The blond had a very defined muscularity only achieved in a gym, and the other had the natural beefiness typical of football players. I attempted to establish some sort of eye contact with either of them until they started chatting up this other girl, at which point I just gave it up.

Of course every damn civilian in the bar hit on me, which only irritated me more. I didn't drive all the way down to Oceanside to find a civilian, and I'm never so desperate that I would settle for leaving with one!

Two a.m. found me outside the bar, unwilling to leave and positively steaming with rage at the prospect of driving home alone, but also feeling pretty stupid and craven for lingering. I was leaning against the wall scanning for a likely Marine. Incredibly, this tall, gawky civilian, who also had been bothering me inside the bar, sidled up and tried to start talking to me again. He asked me if I wanted to go for a walk.

"No, I don't want to go for a walk! Go away!"

The three Marines caught my attention again. They were outside the bar, having a loud drunken exchange with some girl who was yelling at them. She'd been pretty much yelling at them all night over some bullshit or other. (This wasn't the one they had been chatting with earlier; she'd left long before—with her boyfriend.)

Suddenly it was clear to me what I needed to do: rescue them. I got my car, pulled up in front of the Spur, and beeped the horn, signaling one of the three to come over. The dark-haired Marine dutifully trotted over. I asked him if he and his buddies needed a ride.

"Where are you headed?"

"Anywhere you like." I love saying that.

They all piled into the car. The blond one, who was the best-looking, got into the backseat, and the dark-haired Marine climbed in beside me. Naturally, he was the drunkest and the loudest of the trio—just what I needed in the front seat of my car. The third one was a rather runty, pock-faced kid who didn't

really fit my picture of what a member of the United States
Marine Corps should look like. He looked more like the awkward kid brother who always tags along.

Once they determined that I knew where Los Pulgas was, the
trio proceeded to ignore me and continue their private conversation about the bitch outside the bar. Apparently she had been
yelling at Gary, the drunk one sitting next to me, and calling him
a jerk. A fair enough observation, I thought, but I wasn't able to
get a word in to say so. His buddies were too busy telling him
that, yes, he was a jerk, and he should have just kept his mouth
shut.

On the way up Interstate 5 to Las Pulgas, Gary at last addressed me personally.

"I need to piss *right now!*"

I pointed out that we were ten minutes from their barracks at
most. Apparently there was no holding it, so I pulled off to the side
of the road to let him out. While he was relieving himself, I
turned to get a better look at the boys in the back seat. Morgan,
the good-looking blond focused his eyes on me long enough to
form a question.

"Why are you giving us a ride, anyway?"

"Because I'm *nice.*"

I glanced out the window to see what Gary was up to, but before
I could face the road again, Morgan leaned forward and kissed me
deeply. I pressed myself as close to him as I could get without
unbuckling my seatbelt. The runty kid, Stewart, was silent, but I
could feel his eyes on me. When Gary finally returned to the car
Morgan slid back into his own seat. Not a word was said about the
kiss as we proceeded on base. But Stewart spoke up for the first
time, suggesting that I join the three of them for beer once we got to
their barracks.

I really didn't think I'd be allowed through the gate, but it wasn't
a problem. They told the sentry I was their designated driver. All I
had to do was show him my license. When we pulled up to their

barracks, Stewart repeated his invitation to hang out and drink beer with them.

The barracks (the first I'd ever visited) looked like a college dormitory, only more utilitarian. Once we got to the room up on the second floor, they flung open the door, woke up the Marine who was sleeping there, and told him to "GET OUT! Go sleep next door!" I felt bad for him, but I didn't find him attractive, so I didn't suggest he could stay. There was one twin bed against the wall and a set of bunk beds. He just literally rolled off the upper bunk, gathered up his bedding, and left without saying a word.

The place was a fucking mess. They must have just gotten back from the field because there were big green bags with all their gear on the floor, half the shit falling out. I went to the bathroom. When I came out Gary was stretched across a twin bed with his shirt off. I went to sit down on a metal-armed conference-room chair. Before I even had a chance to play along with the charade that I was only there for "the beer" he said, "Want to sit here next to me?" and patted the bed.

You only need to ask once.

I looked at him for a moment, taking in his naked chest and broad shoulders. I reached to stroke his hair and leaned in to kiss him, that's when all hell broke loose. They all came at me at once and started pulling off my clothes and their own. They were each kissing me and grabbing me all over until we were all completely naked. Gary and Morgan both had nice-sized cocks that were already rock-hard. The third Marine, Stewart, was, as I said, a bit scrawny. Not someone I would have ever fucked if the other two hadn't been there. They were determined to make sure that their buddy got some of the action, in that same way you look out for the kid brother who always tags along but can never quite manage things for himself. I figured two hunky Marines made up for one runty one, so I shrugged and let it happen. Besides, he never did fuck me, because his pencil-dick wouldn't get hard—because, he said, the two other guys were there.

The surprising thing, though, is just how comfortable the three of them seemed together, particularly Gary and Morgan. I asked them at one point if they'd done something like this before. They said no, but I'm not sure I believe them. They were just *too* comfortable laughing and joking when saying, "Dude, get your dick out of my face."

Once I started sucking cock, Gary wouldn't kiss me on the mouth but my Irish blond babe, Morgan, had no such problem. I went back and forth between sucking cock and kissing him for quite some time while he was fucking me. The dynamics of their little group put him in charge. He was bossy as hell, to Gary and Stewart as well as to me, telling them what positions were going to be taken next, for which activity, and exactly what I was going to be doing to whom. As my two-and-a-half hours in the room progressed, Morgan came to the decision that he wanted me all to himself and eventually just stopped sharing. At one point I was on top of him, and he pulled me closer and said, "I just want to look at your face." A bit later, after being fucked by Gary for awhile, I laid back against the other two Marines while Morgan fucked me again. We were kissing deeply and essentially ignoring the other two altogether until Gary got pissed and said, "Stop kissing her already, I want her to suck my dick!" And then, "He's gone all romantic. Don't fall in love with the chick!" It was hysterical, as much for the fact that there was no way Morgan was giving me up despite whatever was said to him, because he was the one IN CHARGE.

Stewart pretty much stayed on the periphery, mostly just sucking my tits and trying to ram his fingers up my ass, which I kept putting a stop to since I had no lube with me and wasn't about to let any of them fuck me up the ass, although Gary repeatedly attempted to do so. There were a few tense moments when I thought he might just ignore my refusal to have anal sex. There would have been absolutely nothing I could have done to prevent him from doing it.

"I'm going to fuck you in the ass."

"No, you are not."

"Oh yes I am!" This went back and forth with him trying to stick it in me until I finally lost my temper.

"Knock it the fuck off!"

I knew it was a major risk, but I wasn't about to consent. I'd already decided that if he wanted to rape me, he was going to have to use violence instead of just bullying me into it. But the moment I yelled at him, he backed off, shrugged with a sheepish grin, and raised his hands in a surrender motion. I kissed him and sat on his cock.

So much had happened in such a short time that it's hard to describe events and my reactions in order, but it was all pretty incredible. The tension that occasionally welled up within me only added to the excitement. I knew going into the situation that the male bonding dynamic might make things get a little rough, and they did. They repeatedly slapped my ass, fucked me hard, and moved me around rapidly, cocks shifting in and out of my mouth and cunt, but they never did anything to actually hurt me. Though it often seemed like they were in full control of the sex, they would immediately submit to any suggestions I made, which wasn't often because I was happy allowing myself to be used. Part of the thrill for me was being the catalyst of their male-bonding experience. There was an erotic charge to knowing that, as far as they were concerned, I was just a body for them to share, especially as this was made apparent by their tendency to talk around me rather than to me.

Once Morgan decided he wanted me all to himself, though, I could feel a tense emotional shift in the room, especially with Gary. He seemed to be getting more and more agitated, and after having made the "going all romantic" gibe, he actually got up and left the room. He did this a few times. He would go out and have a smoke, then come back in and try to get near me. Morgan and I were too absorbed with each other to pay him much mind, but I knew it was pissing him off. He got progressively louder, banging his forearms on the walls, hooting and hollering, even out in the hallway, apparently intent on waking up the whole barracks. At one point, he returned to the room with another Marine in tow. I looked up and saw two others outside the door watching, afraid to come inside. Gary grinned at me broadly, pushed the fourth Marine in front of him, and declared "Got a new recruit for ya." He whacked the kid on the back. Morgan had moved away from me a bit at this point, and I was just lying there looking at this new Marine.

For what felt like an entire minute I considered spreading my legs again and letting the new guy fuck me. I told him to lean toward me and I touched his face, considering. But then something clicked. I just knew that Gary was waiting for my assent, and that if I let this Marine stick his cock in me, the two others waiting outside would be next. And while they all took their turns, he would be off gathering more "recruits" to fuck the barracks whore. At that point I virtually pushed Morgan off me. I got up and started looking for my clothes. Rummaging in the dark, I started to feel panicked as I picked up bits of clothing that weren't mine. All four of them started whining.

"What are you doing? You aren't leaving, are you?"

Gary said, "She's not leaving. We're not done with her yet."

That was my cue to turn on the lights! I quickly found most of my clothes. I jammed myself into them and whispered to Morgan, trying to convince him to leave with me and come up to Los Angeles. He wanted me to go to his room. I finished dressing. The two of us left the others and moved next door.

"I'm glad I finally have you all to myself," he told me.

We kissed. He pushed my head down. I sucked his cock. He passed out.

I snuck out of the room and made my way back to my car.

Driving off the base and passing the sentry shack, I fantasized about pulling over and asking the sentry if he would let me blow him. My body was aching and even my lips were dry and cracked

from the constant forceful cocksucking, but some part of me still
wanted more.

It took me an hour and a half to get home, but it didn't feel like
such a long drive. I was elated and kept replaying the entire night
over and over again in my head, expanding on it and letting it
grow into different fantasies. I thought about what would have
happened if I had let that fourth Marine climb on top of me. I
pictured myself lying there on that tiny bed as one Marine after
another lined up to fuck me. Just one endless line. The idea
excited me, but I was not sure my body could take it. Of course
that in itself was part of the turn-on: the prospect of losing control. There had been so many opportunities for things to get out
of hand. I could have let Gary fuck me up the ass, and if I had I'm
sure the others would have wanted to use my asshole as well. I
fantasized about them bending me over the bed and holding me
down while each took his turn in my ass, shooting me full of
"young, dumb," U.S.M.C. come—leaking out and lubricating
my butt for the next cock. I regreted not having lube and more
condoms with me. I regreted not letting that nameless fourth
Marine fuck me senseless until getting off and letting the fifth
and sixth waiting outside the door do the same. . . .

I tell you one thing I don't regret anymore, though, and that's
letting that idiot staff sergeant slip through my fingers as he ran
off to chat up some skank. I bet his night wasn't nearly as good as
mine.

−14−

The Marine Wife

Devon

Jacksonville, North Carolina, had the smallest airport I had ever flown into, and I had been in a lot of airports. It was just one long brick building, nothing more. Perhaps three gates and a coffee shop. Very few ticket counters.

Mike was waiting for me when I deplaned. There was just enough time to pick up the rental car and get to Camp Lejeune before he had to report for formation.

The road was pleasantly desolate in a back-country way, with sparse patches of scrub pines here and there. We passed clumps of primitive wooden shacks with exotic names like "Miss Delilah's All-Female Revue." Mike said they served as whorehouses.

"Off limits of course," he told me. "Yet they still manage to stay in business. You should see their 'World Famous Fishermen's Wharf.' It's a steak house and strip club next to a slough. We'll drive by it later, and I'll show you."

Mike couldn't stop smiling. The smile was broad, open, and very happy. His sharp blue eyes shone with pleasure when I put my hand behind his head the way I always did, to stroke the supershort, fine bristles of dark blond hair. Like the others in his unit, he had been horribly bored since returning to Lejeune after the Norway cold weather exercise.

"We're butt fairies now," he told me. "We pick up litter on base. Our primary purpose is to support the Jacksonville economy, to keep it from collapsing since so many Marines were deployed to the Gulf. So basically there is absolutely nothing for us to do. We're going through the motions, stepped-up PT, etcetera. I'll be happy to start staff NCO school next month. Right now my platoon's keeping busy shooting a motivational video."

The war had been over for two months. The unit's command had been tight-lipped about going home, although rumors were rampant that a date had long since been set. A handout had been passed around among the troops showing an enlisted man in a baby carriage being pushed by an officer. The CO was not happy. The long Easter-weekend leave had been granted partly to stem the unit's growing tide of unrest.

The chow hall's offerings—all classic Southern cuisine—repelled Mike, compounding his unhappiness. "I would kill for some satay," he told me. "They'd deep-fry breakfast if they could." My Marine had developed a more sophisticated palate since our marriage.

"Poor baby," I said, smiling. "There must be some good places to eat off base."

"There's pizza—there's always pizza, everywhere—and El Mex, which is like El Torito. And the Golden Corral, which is like Sizzler. Maybe a little better. I'm glad we're going to visit Wilmington. Maybe there'll be something decent to eat there. You know, they even deep-fry hamburgers here. I didn't know that was possible."

Despite our banter, we both felt strange being around each other again. We'd been apart long enough that we were no longer familiar with each other, a common side effect of military separations. Before Mike had been activated, we were together so much that I lost sight of myself as anything other than one-half of a couple. It had not been a difficult transformation for me. To get married, I had buried parts of myself that I was sure were not conducive to married life. Parts of me that were a little too offbeat, especially for what I imagined Mike expected in a proper, middle-class Marine wife.

I was also uneasy because, during our separation, those parts of me had slowly re-emerged, and I was enjoying them. I was feeling like myself again, but that self was far from what I believed a Marine wife should be. It was rangy, rough, and aggressively erotic, the same wild and hungry self who had prowled the city for sex when I had been single, going and getting just what it wanted. I had gazed at men on the streets, on buses, in bookstores, cafes, and coffeehouses. I admired them, fantasized about them, picked them up, and took them home with me. It usually didn't take more than a smile, a hello, and the offer of a beer back at my apartment. I was not unusually beautiful, but I was ready, willing, available, and self-assured. Few men could resist that.

I projected a sexual aura so strong that I drew men to me: like the tall, wiry blond who spotted me the minute he walked into the cafe and sat at my table; the short, well-dressed Sicilian who turned around and followed me for blocks before we stopped to talk; and the cute, compact, muscled athlete with close-cropped hair who passed me his phone number after a lengthy flirtation on the bus. Later he told me I was the first woman he had wanted in years. There had been days when I barely stepped out of my apartment building before I met a man and went back in again.

It was the self I'd been struggling with since I was eleven. My very strong sexual appetite and the strange, often frightening serenity that accompanied all my efforts to satiate it. It was my most primal and animalistic self—the part of me that liked exploring men, touching them and tasting them, often in very rough ways. The part of me that felt especially close to those male friends with whom I didn't sleep, but instead shared not only a taste for men but for certain sexual practices: licking, sucking, biting, slapping, spanking, pinching, and fucking. Yes, I fucked men, with tongue, fingers, dildo, and fist.

My favorite lovers had been military men. They were the least afraid of my unbridled sexuality; in fact, they welcomed it. Among the military men, I loved Marines best. They were physically the most beautiful, and they smelled and tasted better than any other men alive. I liked their hard bodies, and I liked penetrating and being penetrated by them. When I went to bed with Marines, I drew strength from their heightened masculinity and institutionalized aggression, as though taking their bodies into mine was a sacramental blessing of my own savage and uncommon self.

When I began sleeping with Marines, it was a revelation to see how accepting they were of my sexuality. I marveled at how fully they responded to me, and how open they were to everything I enjoyed doing with a man, regardless of how wild or unusual. I loved the blissful looks on their faces when I touched them in ways many other men had found repellent. I was enraptured with their endless desire for pleasure. "I love making love with you," whispered Jeff, a young corporal, on our second night together as I rode on top of him, leaning down to pinch and bite his nipples, making him shudder all the more. "You love to fuck, don't you? You love it more than anything, don't you?" moaned Roger, the commanding officer of a ship's Marine Detachment, as our bodies moved violently to mesh, our flesh slapping together. Kevin, a sergeant, more than any of the others gave himself to me completely, opening himself up to my gathered, loving fist.

I wanted to marry a Marine, but the wildest and most sexual couldn't be wed. I wanted to at least try to live a "normal" life with a husband, home, and children. I met Mike, who was in the Marine Reserves, had a good civilian job, and also wanted to settle down. He was bright, funny, warm, blessedly emotionally stable, and very kind. I had not experienced much stability or genuine kindness from the men in my life, so I let Mike fall in love with me, and I fell in love with him loving me.

Mike was nothing like the Marines I had known. He was not comfortable with my past or my more eccentric sexual tastes. I turned my back on my old life and began to bury those parts of me not acceptable in my new role. I took those wild parts of myself and placed them in a box, then placed that box inside another box, and another, and another, until so deeply buried that at times I had no feelings at all. I became a very good Marine wife, one much admired for her gung-ho spirit and unfailing support of her husband.

Glimmers of my old self had briefly re-emerged on certain occasions during the three years of my marriage. I couldn't go to the annual Birthday Ball without getting deeply aroused by all those beautiful buzzed-cut young men in their dress blues. Nostalgic, I'd get hot and bothered as I talked and danced with them, thinking of their steely bodies beneath those uniforms. All the wonderful hard Marine bodies I'd had in the past but never would have again. That poignant ache mercifully, lasted only the duration of the ball. Afterward it was tucked down deep again, dormant, yes, but not a little restive.

That ache re-emerged full-time after Mike was deployed, and my ferocious sexual hunger was reborn. I looked at men again for the first time in years, at hands and mouths and asses. Old desires washed over me.

Now I was going to my very first Marine Base. I would be surrounded by the best men of all: Marines with their special scent of Niagara spray starch, cheap vending-machine laundry soap, testosterone, and sweat. (Enlisted Marines smelled that way, at least. Officers, who usually professionally laundered their utilities, rarely smelled as good.)

I immediately found Camp Lejeune a special and beautiful place. On that first day I saw the more manicured parts of the base, all rolling lush green lawns and red brick colonial buildings with white trim, and the inevitable concrete barracks. Mike and I drove past steam vents that alternately moaned and whinnied: the best of these became favorites of mine. Mike indulged me several times during that long weekend, driving up to them and stopping so I could roll down the window to listen. "It's so easy to keep you entertained," he laughed, "you're a cheap date." Later Mike showed me the rougher parts—all dense forests of scrub pines bisected by tank trails. A large swamp-like lake was rumored to be filled with alligators. Another road would take us to a handsome beach with spartan but attractive cabins on stilts.

Mike had his own room in the staff NCO barracks, which was one of the more contemporary structures on base, probably dating to the early 1960s. All the doors of the big, brown dormitory *cum* motel faced out onto balconies running the length of the three-storied building. He carried my bag upstairs to the third floor and proudly led me into his well-equipped room, the largest he had ever had in the military.

He had just enough time left to change into his utilities for formation. All the extra PT had done him good: his belly, chest, arms, and thighs were firmer than before. I laid down on the bed and admired him openly.

"Flex your biceps for me," I told him. Mike grinned and did so. I got up from the bed and happily squeezed that warm, round knot of muscle. He leaned forward and kissed my cheek. He took his utilities blouse from the hanger and pulled the long sleeves over those biceps, hiding them from my admiring eyes. He buttoned up his blouse and tossed me the room and rental-car keys as he put on his cover: "Just in case you want to visit the Exchange."

I kissed him goodbye at the door. "Now remember," he told me, "you're not really supposed to be here, so be discreet." I smiled and nodded, then locked the door behind him. I waited a few minutes, grabbed my purse and the keys, and headed downstairs. I drove to the Exchange and idly shopped, picking up a bathing suit, two Marine Corps coffee mugs, three boxes of chocolate babies (a candy now rarely seen outside the South, but long a favorite of mine), and a pair of black canvas tennis shoes. I waited in the check-out line behind a painfully young Marine just back from the Gulf. He couldn't stop gazing around in bewildered pleasure.

"I can't get over all the colors," he gushed to the poker-faced saleswoman. "They just jump out at you. Everything was so brown in the desert. . . ."

I watched him leave as I paid for my purchases. In another lifetime I would have gone after him, talked to him, gotten to know him. I would have done my utmost to make him comfortable with me so I could gather him close and kiss away the furrows in that young brow, melt away all that sad confusion with my body.

I got lost on the way back to the barracks and had trouble navigating the European circle. When the base policeman started to follow me with lights flashing, I used my standard traffic-ticket-diversion tactic of appearing unaware of his presence while slowly leading him where I wanted to go, so I could then plead ignorance of being pursued. A transport of Marines drove by this spectacle, laughing and shouting, "Lady, they got you!" I smiled mischievously back at them before pulling into the parking lot of the staff NCO barracks.

A brief interrogation followed, "Didn't you see my lights flashing?" "Oh, were you chasing me? I didn't hear any siren. . . ." The gaunt and rigid figure with too-long mustache closely examined my ID card, driver's license, and car rental agreement. In the end, he reacted as every other policeman had. With obvious exasperation at my apparent obliviousness to my many traffic violations, he issued me nothing more than a stern reprimand. Feeling triumphant, I headed back up to the room.

I put my purchases on the desk and turned on the rental television Mike had opted for in lieu of a phone. A quick channel surf confirmed what he'd already told me: "It's nothing but *The Cajun Cook* and endless reruns of *The Andy Griffith Show*. Remember how you told me each city has its own TV series? How in Manhattan it's *The Honeymooners* and in Queens it's *All in the Family?* Well, it's *The Andy Griffith Show* here, and probably for the entire state of North Carolina. . . ."

I turned off the television and lay down on the wide bed. I looked around the strange, institutional room. It was all gray: gray walls, gray lockers (three, an abundance of lockers for an enlisted man, a fact that made Mike especially proud), gray wardrobe, gray desk, gray television. I thought of all the Marines who had stayed in this room, slept between these much-laundered sheets, and wondered if any of them had ever hidden away here a woman like me.

Every so often I heard voices—sharp, male voices, shouts, a devil-dog bark or two outside, and occasionally the soft, deep rumblings of conversation from other rooms. I imagined catching those voices with my own and holding them in my throat, thinking of the throats of the men with those voices. How much I wanted to press my lips and tongue to each neck as they all stood neatly at attention, in rows of one long, endless formation. I slowly undressed each one, conducting my own personal inspection of biceps, chests, bellies, thighs, asses, and of course cocks of all sizes and shapes.

I thought about all the Marines who had ever been through that wonderfully cloistered world of Camp Lejeune. There had been a long, empty road leading in from the main gate, so long and barren that when the first cluster of buildings had appeared, it had seemed as though this very special all-Marine enclave was somehow wonderfully cut off from the outside world. That sense of being enclosed in an environment wholly different from the outside world had only heightened my growing feelings for the Marines who lived and worked there. I closed my eyes and thought about those numberless Marines until I could almost smell them, taste them, and feel their firm muscles under my hands.

I thought of the individual Marines I'd seen in my life, in dress blues on parade, in Charlies on leave in the streets of the city, and in utilities at the Reserves center. I thought of the Marines I'd wanted, like tall, red-haired Butch, the model-handsome Marine I had been talking to the night I had met Mike. Butch might have made my life very different had he been the one who went home with me. Chris, a devastating, dark-eyed, dark-haired member of my husband's platoon, had been as in love with me as I was with him, although we'd never acted on it. I thought of the Marines I'd had the pleasure of sleeping with: Kevin, Roger, Jeff, Rick, Steve, and Greg among them. All very different: tall, short, dark, fair, officer, enlisted, quiet, outgoing, and yet all sharing that same inner strength and self-assur-ance, that cocky sensuality that made Marines unique among the men I had known.

Building, now, I saw that endless formation—this time made up not of faceless strangers but of every Marine I had ever seen, every Marine I had ever wanted, and every Marine I had ever slept with—all now lying naked on some vast parade deck, head to toe in long neat lines while I, equally naked, crawled panther-like from body to body, manlike in my lust and abandonment as I touched, probed, licked, sucked, pinched, spanked, and bit the salty flesh of every last one of them.

I felt that same boundless desire which had been buried so deep inside me re-emerge, prompted not only by the images in my mind but by the sights, sounds, and smells of that barracks surrounded by that vast base designed just for the sort of men I liked most in the world. This was a very different on-base feeling than I'd felt in my monthly excursions to the Reserves Center to photocopy and dis-tribute the unit newsletter I edited. That had been a sense of security every time I entered the gates of the naval base, a feeling of safety in a remote enclave, the sensation that once I was behind those gates nothing could touch me, no one could harm me. I felt softly feminine and protected, passive and safe at last.

Now I tuned into the male voices on either side of me. I felt long-banked savage and combative desires well up in me until I was almost beside myself awaiting the sound of a key in the door that would signal the return of my very own Marine.

And then he was back, knocking at the door, and I let him in and faced the reality of my husband. Mike was hungry and wanted to go out for dinner. He couldn't see all that I was feeling. I watched him shave and shower in the locker-room style concrete bathroom, find-ing new pleasures in gazing very frankly at the line of hair down his belly, the rock-hard thighs, and the beautifully proportioned cock with its perfectly shaped head.

All of a sudden I wasn't looking at my husband, a man who didn't approve of my past and perhaps even feared it, but at a body, a body I wanted to possess like I'd possessed others. A near-perfect male body, a physical ideal, a thing to capture, worship, and enjoy.

Mike had barely finished toweling off when I came up behind him, slid my hands up his chest, and gnawed on his shoulder.

"Well," he murmured, "we can always eat later."

He laid back on the bed and watched me peel off socks, jeans, shirt, bra, and panties. I did that panther-like crawl up his body, enjoying his soapy-fresh scent, the slightly damp skin. I had him exactly how I wanted him. I was ready to possess him in a way that felt more male than female to me.

I kissed, licked, and even bit him. He trembled like legions of men before him had. I mapped his body with my fingers and tongue, tracing every furrow, every crevice, until I got to that most secret part of him. He recoiled when he felt my tongue there. It had been a long time, not since before we were engaged, and he may have not been sober the one time it happened.

Mike flinched again, and then he moved away, his face flashing a look all too familiar, a mixture of embarrassment, disgust, and veiled fear. Each time that expression had filled me with so much pain I had frozen up and lost all desire. This time I got angry. That anger fed my lust with the same barbaric ferocity I had felt for so many men, and had felt with all the other Marines I had ever slept with.

I became like a warrior myself, furiously aggressive and belligerently sexual. I climbed over him and lowered myself down on his upright cock. I fucked him in the only way he'd let me, since he had refused to let me inside him, into the heart of him; refused to let me take him in the way I loved most—with tongue, fingers, and fist.

I was quiet while I fucked him, unusual for me, but we were trying to be discreet since I wasn't supposed to be there. It was a deceptive quiet, however, because I felt vicious and warlike as I rode him, which amplified my pleasure tenfold. I got hotter and wetter than I had been in years, and each downward thrust on that deliciously thick prick felt more exquisite than the last.

As I slid slickly up and down I heard once again the deep, masculine voices of the other Marines all around us, voices in the other rooms, on the landing outside, down below in the parking lot, and in my own throat, until I felt all those voices were indistinguishable from my own. I came that way, and Mike came too, wondering just what had gotten into me.

We showered, dressed, and went to dinner. The rest of the long weekend passed uneventfully. We had dinner in the officer's club the next day with his platoon commander, drove to Wilmington on Saturday and stayed the night there, and enjoyed an Easter Sunday brunch at the Wilmington Hilton.

On Monday we went to one of the many Saigon Sam's surplus stores, enormous Quonset warehouses filled with the uniforms and paraphernalia I enjoyed as much as Mike. "I'm going to have a cartoon drawn of you," he told me with pride and satisfaction as we exited the store together. "You in a jeep, towing a missile behind you and saying, 'Now THAT'S what I call a surplus store!' "

By then I had become more recognizable to him. I had blended back into one-half of our functioning unit together, and it was almost as though we hadn't been apart. I had become Mike's perfect Marine wife again, and all was right with the world.

April first arrived. Heaters were mercifully turned off at last (it had been close to eighty all weekend), air conditioners were turned on, and sleeves went up all over the base. I felt lovely prickles at the sight of all those exposed biceps, but I buried those feelings deep inside me. Mike took me back to the airport, and we were parted once more.

15

In a German Peep Show

Steven Zeeland

Frankfurt, West Germany, 1989—the Red Light District

Today is end-of-month payday. Already at seven o'clock many of the soldiers are trashed. I fall in behind two of them, study their faces in profile as they shout conversation at each other, admire especially the swagger of the one on the right in tight new black Levis, W 34 L 30, shaking his meaty American ass, chomping on a bratwurst. A piece of it breaks off and falls to the sidewalk. A pudgy middle-aged Greek barker steps forward to implore, "Come to us, gentlemen, we have LIFE-SHOW!" The GI offers him the butt of the sausage. The Greek declines but, beaming, thanks him heartily. He seems to think the gesture sincere.

Somehow I feel sorry for him. And for the leather-faced Turk grandpa in fez who comes up and stands close beside me my first few minutes in Dr. Müller's peep-show. Wordlessly he indicates the videocassette cover display case before us and grins, flashing surprisingly healthy white teeth. I smile back, out of charity. Encouraged, he pantomimes jerking off. I frown. He points at a gay video cover, questioningly, brown eyes wide like a child's. I shake my head again, but I am no longer looking at him. He recedes.

When I'm in my voyeur mode, I try to avoid any unnecessary human contact. Really, I want to be invisible, a goal that, however unattainable, I've lately begun to feel myself edging closer to.

Dr. Müller's is the cleanest and most deluxe of Frankfurt's *wix-fabriken*—masturbation mills—with row upon row of 240-channel video booths, a girlie show rotunda, a DJ booth, and attendants in white boiler suits resembling pilot fishes on sharks phlegmatically policing sperm.

Benny beckons me to the change counter. He is a skinny Basque in his twenties whose long, scraggly hair and severe raccoon eyes prompted one unnerved GI to comment, "*Fuck,* man! Alice Cooper motherfucker." He wants to ask me something. "Do you have ID card? Can you buy in PX?" Germans are always asking me to procure them the craziest things. Scuba diving equipment. Powdered eggs. Disney memorabilia. And they assume that these items will be as good as free. Benny only wants a bottle of Southern Comfort. I tell him it will be ten marks. This is a good price; but, as he probably expects, chances are I will end up just giving it to him for free, as a bribe. We shake on it. Pleased, he asks me if I'd like anything to drink. He pours me out a plastic shot glass of Asbach brandy, and reflects, "*Ja ja,* we are all just horny young rams here."

This is unusually direct. Most of the employees at Dr. Müller's know about my activities and don't appear to care. But as one of them once commented, "That doesn't mean it has to be talked about."

I ask Benny what's new. He leans forward: "On Wednesday we found a *fixer* in one of the cabins—dead! That makes the fourth corpse since I am working here."

I act jaded. "But always junkies. Never a murder."

He gives me a wounded look. "No, *but:* once two guys came up the stairs carrying a third. They told me I should call him an ambulance. I thought at first the man was drunk. Then I saw that his shirt was covered with red. 'Have a look,' said the guy who was carrying him. He tipped back the head to reveal a fully sliced-open throat, and exposed, still-pulsing veins. 'Get him out of here!' I told them. 'This is not a hospital. Call your own ambulance.' Like spaghetti, it looked. The guy was ready to die right there," he concludes, his inky eyes staring deep into mine as he lowers his mouth to the microphone, raises the peg on the mixer and impressively intones, *"Live dabei sein!*—haff a look!—*wir haben freie Kabinen*—vee haff free cabins—*in fünf Minuten Lesbe Show*—*und jetzt Modelwechsel:* and now vee change ze girl."

I once tried to tell a pornjay that he should say "booth" instead of "cabin."

A Rastafarian dwarf comes up the stairs blowing on a harmonica. I'd noticed him earlier in the train station "B" level, busking for coins, playing "Heart of Gold" even as only a few meters away leather-clad *Polizei* with *deutsche schäfer* dogs were beating some unfortunate with billy clubs.

Benny yells out, "Be still, you half-portion!" He calls for the cleaner fish to bring out a stool so that the man can watch the simulated lesbian sex show.

"All men come to Dr. Müller's," I observe.

Benny nods with conviction. "That is really true. Since I am working here I have seen many well-known people . . ." He reels off a list of names, mostly German TV personalities, politicians, and the like. I politely pretend to listen while at the same time monitoring the movements of a young man who has just come up the stairs and now stands looking at the Polaroids of the models. With his dark hair, olive skin, and European clothes he looks like an Italian but for his Army regulation haircut and moustache. When he steps into the life-show I offer Benny a sheepish smile. He grants me a patronizing nod as I take my leave to investigate.

Because the booth I'm in is in Benny's view, and because all the other booths are occupied, I drop in a mark. Ignoring the unscrolling curtain, I squat down (the floor is too wet to kneel on) and peer through one of multiple illicit peepholes that have been drilled into the thin particle-board partition.

White hands unzip black trousers and free a semi-erect uncircumcised penis of average length with foreskin partially retracted. It hangs about five inches away from the peephole. After a moment, to my surprise, with forced, violent spurts it starts to *piss.* Now the fingers play with the foreskin, pulling it up and down, shaking out drops of urine; now begin tugging more rhythmically. The penis is fully erect; the shiny purple head with its wet *schlitz* aimed more or less directly at my eye. I drop in another mark as, abruptly, the hands zip up.

The booth is empty.

Masturbatory techniques of the American fighting man. Thousands of soldiers and airmen blur and fade. What sticks in my memory is the unusual. The cowboy with the long sideburns and Wrangler jeans whose meatus swallowed the first joint of his pinkie, but when he reached orgasm he masturbated the ordinary way. The ruddy-complexioned guy in the maroon Fruit-of-the-Looms who shot off three times at five-minute intervals without a break. The tall, hung blond in a letter jacket who stood in a life-show booth, hands at his sides, and without touching himself loosed a long ropy white filament. But the GIs who lick up their own ejaculate, transferring even the last squeezed after-come from finger to tongue have long since become too numerous to remember.

Tonight I watch a tough old sergeant with an enormous TEXAS belt buckle masturbate with quick, spastic jerks, dribbling just a few meager drops onto a McDonald's napkin. In contrast, an anonymous—no face-level hole has been bored in this booth—beautiful pink circumcised penis shoots off copiously ("Like a fountain!" a stocky German known among the cruisers as Rumpelstiltskin emerges hyperventilating from the other side and pantomimes to his cruising sister, a balding Turk I call "Null Null," after a German brand of toilet disinfectant); when the stall door opens I am unnerved to match this dream penis with a Turk with a hideously disfigured nose (the *schönste schwänze* often come paired with the ugliest faces). A redheaded Air Force guy, seated, spurts arterial pulses against the inverted cup of his palm. He flings it at the wall and wipes his fingers on his socks. I tail him into the men's room where I steal a view of his still swollen penis, a few clumps of semen in the stream of his urine. A gawky soldier with Army-issue "birth control" glasses and saggy-butt orange-tag Levis just plays with himself for a bit then puts it away and leaves. (Some men beat off for a half hour or longer but never come; others spend a hundred or more marks and never even touch themselves.) A freckle-faced first-timer in a black nylon jacket labeled Winchell Auto Parts, Winchell, Nebraska has just opened his fly when his buddy starts pounding on the door, it's time to go.

Finally, I watch the sausage-eater in thirty-four-inch waist Levis who I had studied earlier on the street. I follow him back down to the doorway and watch until he disappears from view.

* * *

A man of about thirty-five stares back at me from across the street. He has short-cropped blond hair and a U.S. Army regulation moustache. He's wearing true American Levis (not the "genuine American Levis" made in Malta for Europeans) and conspicuously holds a small plastic Stars and Stripes bookstore shopping bag. My critical eye zeroes in on the telltale German basketball shoes he wears, an expensive brand sold "on the economy" and not in the PX. And whenever I see this guy it is always with the same shopping bag. We scowl at each other. But really we are not competitors: I know he is watching for any GI who might stray into Kino 6, Dr. Müller's basement big-screen theater, the one marked "GAY." My turf is two floors up.

My smugness evaporates when I see a more threatening creature approaching behind him. "George Bush" advances up Kaiserstrasse high on canned Henninger Export *bier,* dressed in a rust down vest and ill-fitting flared jeans of a brand discontinued a decade before and not yet rehabilitated by fashion miscreants. He stops to exchange information with the faux-GI, who points in my direction. I flee back upstairs, but soon have no choice but to helplessly watch as Bush's triangular-shaped head and strong, spiny front legs ascend Dr. Müller's stairs. I frown as I see Benny greet him. He advances on me.

"Well, you're in your usual spot, I see."

I smile, grimly. Bush, who looks like a monster movie cross between the president and a praying mantis, has an uncanny knack for materializing simultaneous with all the most desirable GIs, the youngest and most vulnerable of whom he plies with alcohol, corners in video cabins, and sucks. He claims he always leaves the boys an escape route, but he admits that few of them are ever seen in the red-light district again. Of course my own strategy of waiting for GIs to signal some kind of interest in *me* doesn't bring quite the same results.

"So what's been going on up here?"

"You haven't missed anything. I did see some hot guy going down into Kino 6," I lie, "but I don't have the thirteen marks to pursue him." I'm hoping that Bush might be encouraged to move to the dark basement cinema—where he belongs. "No, I think it's going to be a very slow evening up here."

"Shit, I hope not. It's end-of-month payday. So you *better* still have thirteen marks left in your wallet!" Since our first meeting, when he sidled up to me with a slurred "You can tell a GI from a mile away," Bush has resolutely refused to accept that I am not in the military.

Our conversation is interrupted by the swaggering entrance of a sturdy, short, white soldier with a Marine-style haircut wearing a tight black T-shirt and an even tighter pair of Levis outlining what looks like a hammer handle. He meets our gaping stares and barks, "What's up?" After exchanging a few crumpled dollars for deutschmarks he struts over to the video cover showcase. If possible, he looks even more sturdy from behind.

In the blink of a compound eye, Bush drops his deceptively humble posture and lurches into pursuit. I glare hotly and follow, prepared if necessary to re-enact a shoving match we once had in which, though much smaller than my opponent, I prevailed through sheer force of conviction, or at least desperation. But abruptly the soldier walks over to the life show and checks into the only booth currently without holes.

"Never a dull moment," says Bush, staggering uninvited back to my spot, his rust down vest blending into the orange-particle board video booth doors with enviable anole aplomb.

"Oh, he was straight."

"Shit, don't make me question your intelligence. That don't mean nothin'. Last week I was in the *kino* downstairs. This cute E-4 told me he was supposed to be bringing his wife a pizza. Actually had the pizza there with him in the movie; I could smell the anchovies. Said he wanted to suck *me*, if you can you believe it. I told him, 'Help yourself!'"

I try to keep from visibly gagging. Master Sergeant Bush, my sources tell me, has another life in Kaiserslautern, "K-town," a city of 100,000 Germans and 72,000 Americans two and a half hours southwest of Frankfurt. A wife, kids. A second car he keeps with German, not U.S. forces, plates that he switches to on the ride up here. I pity him and feel guilty for hoping he'll fall asleep on the *autobahn.*

A tall, mean-looking GI comes up the stairs. I recognize him as a soldier who several weeks previous had caught me looking at him and responded with a sustained, smoldering "fight me or fuck me" stare. I'd followed him around the red light district, even to Mayer Gustl's Bavarian Bierhaus, but nothing had happened.

He sees me now but pretends not to, and marches over to the life-show Polaroids. His high-and-tight haircut, an elliptical "pussy patch" of dark wiry bristles capping side scalp shorn bare, exposes the hard insistent form of the head. He sports "snug-seat, relaxed-thigh" Levis, a striped PX rugby shirt, "topsiders" with no socks, and what appears to be an ankle bracelet, an unfamiliar touch that hardly promises deviation, probably just some new stateside convention as dully conformist as the ubiquitous (although/because forbidden on base) pierced left ear.

"This one," I nod to Bush.

"Which one?" Bush scans the boy. He shrugs, meaning that he doesn't register any ultrasonic indication of prey. I reflect that I didn't know what I was doing in pursuing the soldier. Neither of us follows him when he moves to a video booth, and just then Private Hammerhandle exits the life show and bounds down the stairs. Bush, in parting, waves grandly over Dr. Müller's. "It's all yours."

*   *   *

Two hours later, George Bush has said goodbye another six or seven times when the rough-looking GI comes up the stairs again. This time he throws me a brief direct look and in his black eyes I almost imagine reproach. He lingers by the video cover display again, but I am determined to ignore him.

Null Null sniffs at and begins to describe a circle around the soldier. He's joined by Rumpelstilstkin, who slides up close beside, shifting his weight from one foot to the other and pulling suggestively on his beard. Out of nowhere a third cruiser I call Fred Flintstone appears and moves in. Alarmed, I walk over and position myself protectively beside the soldier. His eyes don't budge from the video case. Is he looking at my reflection? Or just his own. Predictably, he walks back over to the life-show area. But just as he is about to step into a booth he veers abruptly back around and heads down the stairs and outside.

I feel a surge.

At the corner where I stood during our initial showdown, he turns right—the direction I had signaled him to head in before he fled to the Bierhaus. I follow, then draw even. For a few paces I walk alongside him, not looking. Then I pass a little ahead.

The Greek barker has abandoned his post outside "Pigalle" and there is no one standing around inside this scummiest of peep shows. The soldier follows me in. I step up to the video display case. The two of us stand side by side. After a half minute I throw him what I hope is an encouraging look and pass down the right side of the video cabin island. He follows close behind. I stop even with the open door of a large booth set perpendicular to the others, out of view from the street and big enough for two. Together, the soldier and I look into the cabin. The floor is a thick pool of urine or other fluid. He brushes past me.

I follow him around the island of booths. We return to the be-fouled party-size stall and stare into it again, as if by some miracle it might have been cleaned in the intervening minute. I walk halfway back around, wait for him to draw even, in a moment of decision open the door on one of the smaller booths and block his path. Authoritatively I nod for him to step in.

He balks. "What?" His tone is harsh. He looks at me and shakes his head. "I ain't never done this before."

I breathe. "Me neither. That is, it's been a while. Come on."

He takes a step back. "No. . . ."

I look at him. "Well, how about— You want to just go walk around some?"

He nods.

I don't stop to ask myself what I'm doing, for once don't critique my strategy. When we are out on the street I ask him, "So where are you from?"

"Iowa."

"How long have you been over here?"

"About two years."

"How do you like Germany?"

"It's all right."

The soldier answers all of my queries in the same clipped fashion. He walks with an exaggeratedly erect carriage, which I, who tend to slouch, half-imitate. This makes me a little taller, and the soldier is tall.

"Are you in the Army?" he asks me his first question.

"No, I'm a civilian. I work for the Army. I'm a clerk, studying to be a translator." This appears to meet with his approval.

In a few minutes we have walked three quarters of the way around the block. Without comment, I turn left on Kaiserstrasse, steering him away from the train station. There is a tense pause.

"I don't live that far from here."

He is silent. I half expect him to bolt, in my nervousness half want to run away myself. But inexorably we march on.

We come to Taunusanlage, part of a ring of park around the city center. I nod, indicating a few shadowy figures lurking above the stairs to a subterranean *Herrentoilette.* "A lot of older gay men cruise there."

"I'm not—" The soldier falters.

"You're not gay, I know."

He says, more confidently: "I like girls. I'm just sort of curious."

"Yeah, I know you like girls," I reassure him. "After all, I saw you looking at them in the peep show!"

He grins. "Yeah, there's one girl there I especially like. She ain't working there tonight though."

A pause. "You know, that first time I saw you, I didn't know whether you were . . . interested or wanted to kick my ass."

Silence.

"How did you know what I . . ."

"Oh, I just figured, in a place like that."

I point out more sights. The statue of Schiller. And, near the Hauptwache, to his amazement, a glass door stenciled "The European Office of The State of Iowa." The soldier doesn't talk much, but I keep up a running banter, and a few times I even get him to laugh. But at the arched stone gateway to my prewar apartment building we both fall silent.

Inside the long skinny entranceway to my room I introduce him to Anja.

"My mom's got cats," he says.

"Do you want a beer? I've got Bitburger Pils, 'the beer that made Bitburg famous.'"

He sits down tentatively at the edge of the bed and looks at my small, multisystem television set. "Do you get MTV?"

I'm grateful that I do. I turn it on. The first thing we see is that crazy Belgian veejay Marcel, dancing around to an ominous sequencer octave bass line in his mop hair, birth control glasses, and plaid vest. "At last Belgian New Beat is getting more heavy, and I love that! It's a really good track, and maybe it's a good track because of the rhythm to tell you a bit more about the AIDS awareness week we gonna have from Monday to next Saturday." Marcel stops dancing long enough to reach off-camera for a long banner depicting a condom and the message COVER YOURSELF AGAINST AIDS. "Because we trying to do something about AIDS here on MTV." He lets go of the banner and it curls up with a snap. "Once you use it, please don't reuse it! T'row it away! T'row it away my friends!" he gesticulates madly. "Yes, very good. Now we have some old music. There was still glitter and glamour in 1978. This is Hot Chocolate and 'Everyone's a Winner,' baby!"

The soldier stares. I murmur uncomfortably, "I guess MTV-Europe is probably a lot different from the States."

I study his features. His square jaw and dark eyes are almost too severe for his face to be called pretty but for his full red lips and pert nose. His hair is black and kinky. I wonder if he is part American Indian, or even African. Awkwardly, it occurs to me to stretch out my hand and say, "My name's Steve."

"Oh," says the soldier, putting down his beer. "Brent."
I can't have heard right. This is the name of the soldier I dropped out of college to follow to Germany.

"Brad?"

"Brent."

He indicates my shelf of videos. "What are all these videos?"

"Oh, European art films, pornos. Holocaust documentaries. Do you want to watch one?"

"What?"

"A porno, I mean."

He shrugs. "I don't care."

For occasions such as this I have a strategically edited straight-bi-gay compilation tape. Because he has told me he's "curious," I decide I can fast forward.

"You ready for another beer?"

He is.

I hit play.

Heart pounding I lay my hand on the inside of the soldier's thigh. He leans back, slightly. I squeeze the crotch of his jeans. He is erect. Slowly, I rub my fingertips up and down alongside the fly, apply more pressure. Tentatively, he reaches his own hand toward me, but just shy of touching me he jerks it back. Moving my hand to his belly I'm surprised at how hard this part of his body is, too. I grab at the rugby shirt and pull it loose from his jeans. His stomach is flat and hairless. I lean down and kiss it; without looking, grab the remote and hit mute. I hate porno soundtracks, and I want to hear the soldier breathing. I put my hand on his chest and push, but he resists, so instead I reach for his belt. He grabs it himself, stands up, and pulls down his pants, revealing those red-and-white striped Jockey briefs you can buy in a plastic tube at the PX. He starts to pull these down but I stop him, make him sit back down. His penis is pinned over to the side; the bright pink head, just poking over the elastic, is wet. I put my mouth to the fabric and feel dizzy.

"What if I come right away?"

Surprised, I answer, "Um, that's—fine." Though I know it's not what he's asking, I add, "Normally I'm really careful about safe sex, but since you've never done this before—You're *sure* you never have, right?"

"Not with a *guy*—"

He breaks off as I pull down his briefs.

Anja watches from atop the bookcase.

I kiss the front of the soldier's penis, just below the head, and press it against my cheek forcefully with the palm of my hand. His scrotum smells faintly of soap. I lick it, taking first one and then both testicles into my mouth. Enraptured, I gaze upon the miraculous beauty of his dick. Having seen so many at the peep show, it takes a lot to impress me. I put my hand around the smooth shaft, and have hardly even given it one saliva-lubed stroke when I notice two small drops of white on his stomach. The soldier gives a little gasp as I bring my mouth down full and suck hard. His semen, too, tastes vaguely soapy. Chasing it with Bitburger, I ask, "Um, can you come again?"

Sex has lasted three minutes.

"I don't know. Maybe."

I go back to work, and he stays hard, but I sense him squirming, and after only a minute he asks what time it is. "I'm gonna have to get going." He pulls up his pants.

I offer him my telephone number. He takes it and says, "I probably won't call you. But I'll probably see you at that place again."

I tell him how he can get back to the train station and offer to walk with him to the stop, but he says, no, he'll find it himself. As he heads down my hallway I recover my humor enough to ask, "So how was it? The first time with another guy."

With a butch nod, he says, in the tone of a man offering praise for a movie he was surprised to like, "It was all right."

The door closes after him. I walk back down my hall, pet Anja and notice there is some beer left in Brent's bottle. I drink it, reasoning that if I have ingested any dangerous microbes maybe the Bitburger will kill them. But I don't feel that I have. I feel euphoric. Even though I know, of course, that I will never see him again. Or, worse, if I do, that he will pretend not to know me.

* * *

The following Friday I have hardly been at Dr. Müller's a half hour when Brent comes up the stairs and gives me a nod. "How are you tonight," he says, as I hurry over to him. "Hold up a sec'."

He steps into the life-show. I resist the impulse to monitor his activity from the neighbor booth. When he comes out we walk down the steps together to the corner. I ask, "So what are you up for tonight? More adventure, or are you just going to the Bier-haus?"

"I don't care. I've got a couple hours. Let's go to your place and watch videos."

And so we do. And it's the same. Except this time, when he tentatively extends his hand my way, I grab it and push it firmly against my penis. And when I get behind him and kiss his neck, he astonishes me by falling backward against me in wild abandon. This time, as we tumble about my narrow single bed kissing and sucking and rubbing, I lose myself.

I ride with him to the *bahnhof.* There's a tense moment on the *U-bahn.* A drunken GI sitting opposite leans over and asks us where we are stationed. Brent is silent. I say, "I'm a civilian."

"Oh," answers the GI with a hurt expression. "Yeah. So am I. I'm the fuckin' ambassador."

At the *bahnhof schnell imbiss,* Brent orders a quarter chicken and asks me to have them cut it for him. For a moment he becomes almost animated as he explains that he was engaged to a German woman but broke it off because "I came here by myself, so I figured I'd go back by myself." His stuff had already been shipped back to the States when he got word that he had been accepted to the elite "jump school" for paratroopers, and was involuntarily extended. With no clear plan he had wandered the streets of Frank-furt. He had seen me at Dr. Müller's, thought about it, and come back looking for me. "I'll be here for another five months," he concludes cheerfully. But when he's about to board the train he looks all stiff and dour again, so I just say, "Okay. See you," and turn around and walk away. Still, I am paranoid enough (How do I know he won't get off the train and head to the bathhouse?) to wait out of view at the end of the track until the train is gone.

Dr. Müller's is still open. Compulsively, I start to walk there. Already across the street I can smell the disinfectant. I surprise myself and keep on walking. Singing.

*   *   *

Brent came back the next week, and the week after. My butch straight soldier ideal was chasing *me*. When I told my neighbor Anna about Brent she was less than enthusiastic.

"I can only say you are in for a lot of trouble if you start making eye contact with people on the street. Watch out that you do not come to grief! It is like I always tell you: you idealize people. Very probably this soldier is just some pathetic swine. Based on your description I imagine him to be like the dumb, horse-tending soldier in the film version of Carson McCuller's *Reflections in a Golden Eye*. I could of course be mistaken, but. . . . And he goes to the Bierhaus! *Oh gott-oh-gott!* As a child of seven or eight I used to go there with my father. Back then, in the early years after the war, it was a decent, *kleinbürgerlicher* place where one could go for a good square meal. There was a big band, which at special times a member of the audience could direct. I remember a handsome American GI who presented me with a large inflatable pig. I think because I directed the band."

16

Tank Trail

Alex Buchman

I'm standing at the end of the Oceanside Pier looking out into the inky night blackness of the Pacific Ocean, trying to work off my beer buzz. Half an hour ago, I had left Jughead's. I had been hanging out there with some of my buddies from my unit, and they all had hooked up and left with overweight bar tramps, and now I was left by myself again. I like watching out for my buddies. Especially the newer guys to the unit, they usually get treated pretty badly by the other Marines. As a lowly corporal in my unit, it's tough for me. I have to watch out for my brother Marines without coming off as too much of a hard-ass. But I love being a Marine and the Marines I serve with. But tonight, it leaves me out on the pier, alone.

A Mexican family is sitting just off to my left. The father is fishing, and his two kids are sleeping curled up together in a blanket on the pier. He gets a bite and reels in a big fish. It's a flounder or some other species of flatfish. I walk over. He grins at me and clubs the creature dead. I decide it's time to leave.

The cool ocean air cuts through my thin flannel shirt and makes me feel confident I'm sober enough to drive. I walk back down the pier slowly, ready for any lost or cruising Marines. Not that I expect to find anything, this being a weekend before payday.

All in all, it was a pretty mellow night out. No big fights, only some playful wrestling in the bar. Still, enough to get me worked up. Oh well. A short jack-off session then to bed after I get back to the barracks.

It's a short walk from the foot of the pier to the block where my car is parked. After passing by and giving a polite "no" to Candy, a notorious local transvestite prostitute that I actually find somewhat attractive, I get into my car and start off to base. Heading toward the Main Gate is my best option since the guards there usually aren't as big of pricks to anyone coming back this time of night.

Driving down Hill Street I notice a young Marine sitting at a bus stop, bound for Camp Pendleton. He is about 6' 1'' and has a nice solid frame, a strongly chiseled face, and a high-and-tight haircut topped with a swatch of dark brown. Since the busses stop running at two-thirty, and it is now three, he is in for a long night of waiting. Without really even thinking about it I stop to offer him a lift.

"Where are you going?"

"San Onofre," he replies in a husky Texan accent as he leans into the open window of my 1994 Nissan Sentra, his big meaty forearms pressing into the doorframe.

"The busses don't run this late. You want a ride?"

He grabs his duffel bag and climbs into my car.

"My name's Alex."

"I'm Trent." I can tell that he's been drinking all night too.

On our way to the base we make Marine small talk. Turns out he's a boot, two weeks from finishing grunt training. Next week, he gets his orders for his first permanent duty station. He says he doesn't have too many complaints. He likes it—"especially the physical part." This catches my attention, but I start to drift a little when he goes on and on about growing up in some small town near Dallas.

"So were you hanging out with your buddies tonight?"

He says that he had been but they all hooked up, and he was left without a ride.

We reach the gate. The sentry waves us through. But Camp Pendleton is a large base, and we're still a half hour away from San Onofre. I'm stationed closer, on the Mainside, but I'm feeling generous and he's a Marine in need.

We talk about the Corps, back home, and growing up. Today was one of the warmest so far this July, and I roll down my window to let the cool night air in. There is the scent of fennel, like black licorice only more subtle. As we drive past the Las Flores area, I catch him looking at me through the corner of my eye. I chalk it up to wishful thinking. But as we pass the Las Pulgas area, a little further up the road, he lets his arm brush up against mine. It feels deliberate. My face flushes. I've heard about gay guys picking up Marines from bus stops, but it's not a game I've ever played. It feels like all the blood in my body is rushing to my dick.

We continue in silence. After we pass Camp Horno, he says he has to piss.

"San Onofre is only a few miles ahead."

"No, I really gotta piss," he says sharply.

I pull off onto a dirt road. I have to piss too. We both get out of the car and stand in front of the car.

I left my lights on. I try to concentrate on pissing but through my semi hard-on I can't. After another uncomfortable silence I dart a sideways glance at Trent. He immediately looks back toward me and turns to face me. His tight, ass-hugging Levis are fully unzipped to expose his white briefs pulled down over his balls and his growing hard-on. He walks in front of the headlights toward me, his cock swinging. He stands a few inches taller than me. I'm toned and fit, but not nearly as beefy as he is.

"I saw your hard-on while you were driving" he says deeply. "I thought we could take care of each other."

I'm speechless. He starts jacking off with his right hand and with his left slowly unbuttons his shirt.

Even though we're at least thirty feet off the road, I take time out to shut off the headlights just in case a bored MP drives by and gets curious. The moon is out and nearly full. Even though the high bushes on either side give us camouflage from the road, I can see the grass-covered hillsides and ravines around us with surprising clarity.

I start jacking off in front of Trent. He's stripped off his shirt to reveal a beautiful chest, defined and smooth. I move to his side. We jack off together with our arms pressed close. His pants keep inching down, first revealing a hairless crack, then his full meaty ass. I've always loved Marines' asses. Whether in PT shorts or Levis, Marines have great asses. I put my hand on one of his ass cheeks and start rubbing it slowly. He starts to sway a little and before I know it, he's on his knees in front of me. He takes my dick in his mouth and starts sucking. But he surprises me again because it's obvious he doesn't have much experience. He keeps raking his teeth along my dick which makes me cringe, but ultimately turns me on even more. He gets more and more into it. I begin thrusting my hips forward and grabbing his ears and he makes noises to encourage me.

I'm getting close. I make him stand up, drop down on my knees. His crotch is musty and slightly damp from a night's worth of being packed into his jeans. I take his dick in my mouth. He moans and pumps his hips more gently than I had. "Suck it, yeah," he says, after five minutes of me sucking on *his* cock.

Pulling me to my feet, he turns around and bends over for me to admire his muscular ass. I caress it slowly, set my dick in the crack, savor the warmth, but get distracted rubbing his back. He whispers, "Fuck me."

It only takes me a second to get my little bottle of lube and a condom from the car. I put it on and place the tip of my rock-hard dick against his hole and gently press forward. He's so tight that I am about to tell him that I don't think this is a good idea, when he relaxes and my dick slips into his ass. Even through the condom I can feel the warmth of his hole. Very, very slowly I pump my cock into his ass until finally I bury myself entirely inside him and feel him shuddering lying across the hood of my car. Building my tempo, I push my forehead into the bristles on the back of his head. He makes soft moaning noises. I put my tongue in his ear. It's obvious no one has ever done this to him before because he jumps so much, and I almost slip out of him. But he stays on the hood and starts chanting, "Fuck, yeah fuck, fuck yeah" in that deep Texan accent of his until he shoots off over the hood of my white car. I pull out, slip the condom off, and come on the ground near our feet.

We dress quickly, get back in the car and don't say much on what's left of the short ride to Camp San Onofre. Outside his barracks, he looks drunker and more tired than he did before as he smiles and murmurs, "Thanks for the ride." I drive off without bothering to ask for a phone number. Leaving, I tell myself: that's all I wanted.

CONTRIBUTORS

Aarek is the pseudonym of an active-duty Danish-American paratrooper.

Alberto is the real name of an enlisted soldier whose present whereabouts are unknown.

Tim Bergling is a TV news producer/freelance journalist who lives and works in the Washington, DC, area. He is a former U.S. Marine sergeant (1982-1990) who was booted out of the Corps for being gay. His writing has appeared in *Genre, Instinct, Hero,* and *Out.* He is currently working on his first book, *Sissyphobia* (Harrington Park Press *Southern Tier Editions,* 2001).

Former Staff Sergeant **Danny** served in the U.S. Air Force from 1977 to 1986. He received two Commendation medals, three Good Conduct medals, and numerous other awards. His military career ended after he was interrogated by the Air Force Office of Special Investigations. He received a general discharge for being gay. He now lives in Kentucky.

Harry Davis was born and raised in Los Angeles. After his military service, he graduated from UCLA and now lives and works in San Francisco.

Devon is the pseudonym of a published author and freelance writer whose work ranges from business newsletters to erotica and pornography. She has been married to a Marine for more than ten years.

Steve Kokker's credits include the short films *Birch (Berioza)* and *Happiness Is a Thing Called Joe;* sharing the big screen with Matt Dillon in Gus Van Sant's *To Die For;* and, most recently, co-authorship of the travel guide, *Estonia, Lativa, & Lithuania* (Lonely Planet, 2000). He divides his time between his native Montreal; Tallinn, Estonia; and St. Petersburg, Russia.

Lewis is the pseudonym of an active duty submariner currently stationed in the Pacific Northwest.

Daniel Luckenbill was drafted into the U.S. Army in 1967. He attended Officer Candidate School, was commissioned 2nd Lieutenant, Field Artillery, and served in Vietnam (1968-1969). He studied writing under Christopher Isherwood, John Rechy, and Elisabeth Nonas at the Institute of Gay and Lesbian Education, West Hollywood, California. His many publishing credits include "As a Marine," anthologized in Ian Young's *On the Line: New Gay Fiction* (Crossing Press, 1981), and an essay featured in *The Isherwood Century* (Wisconsin, 2000). He chairs the Steering Committee of the UCLA LGBT Faculty/Staff Network. He lives in Hollywood.

San Francisco native **Bob Serrano** is an artist, consultant, naval historian, and storyteller.

Matt Bernstein Sycamore is the editor of *Tricks and Treats: Sex Workers Write About Their Clients* (The Haworth Press, 2000). His writing has appeared in *Best American Gay Fiction 3, Best Gay Erotica 2000, Obsessed, Flesh and the Word 4,* and other publications. He is currently at work on an anthology, *Dangerous Families: Queer Writing on Surviving Abuse,* and a collection of short stories, *Sketchtasy.* He lives in New York City.

Steven Zeeland is the author of four books on homoeroticism in the military, all published by The Haworth Press. He is a

Research Associate at the Center for Research and Education in Sexuality (CERES) at San Francisco State University. His work has appeared in *The Face,* the *Village Voice,* and *The Times* (London). He is the subject of the song "Steven Zeeland" by the recording artist Momus. Zeeland's Web sites can be accessed at <www.stevenzeeland.com> and <www.seadogphoto.com>.